SENTIMENTAL

Reader's Digest
PIANO LIBRARY

Journey

WITHDRAWN
FROM THE RECORDS OF THE
MID-CONTINENT PUBLIC LIBRARY

SONGS THAT WON THE WAR ARRANGED FOR PIANO AND VOICE

Project Editor: David Bradley
Cover design by Josh Labouve
Cover photograph © Getty Images
Master recordings supplied by kind permission of Reader's Digest Music

Exclusive Distributors:
Music Sales Corporation
257 Park Avenue South, New York, NY 10010, USA
Music Sales Limited
14-15 Berners Street, London, W1T 3LJ, England
Music Sales Pty. Limited
20 Resolution Drive, Caringbah, NSW 2229, Australia.

Order No. AM993960
ISBN: 978.0.8256.3645.5

Printed in the United States of America by
Vicks Lithograph and Printing Corporation

Amsco Publications
A Part of **The Music Sales Group**
New York/London/Paris/Sydney/Copenhagen/Berlin/Tokyo/Madrid

COMPACT DISC
TRACK LISTING

Disc 1

1. All Or Nothing At All (Lawrence/Altman)
   Gordon Langford, His Piano and Orchestra

2. As Time Goes By (Hupfield)
   Jo Stafford, vocal; Paul Weston and His Orchestra

3. Dream (Mercer)
   Steve Clayton, vocal; Roland Shaw, His Orchestra and Chorus

4. I'm Beginning To See The Light
   (George/Hodges/Ellington/James)
   Helen Forrest, vocal; Harry James and His Orchestra

5. It's Only A Paper Moon (Arlen/Rose/Harburg)
   The Four Barons, vocals; Ray Monk and His Orchestra

6. Let's Fall In Love (Koehler/Arlen)
   Peter Knight and His Orchestra

7. Long Ago (And Far Away) (Gershwin/Kern)
   Beverly Kelly, vocal; Alan Copeland and His Orchestra

8. Mairzy Doats And Dozy Doats
   (Hoffman/Drake/Livingston)
   Dorothy Collins, vocal; Raymond Scott and His Orchestra

9. Moonglow (Hudson/DeLange/Mills)
   Les Brown and His Band of Renown

10. Moonlight In Vermont (Suessdorf/Blackburn)
    Gordon Langford and His Orchestra

11. The More I See You (Gordon/Warren)
    Tex Beneke, sax; and His Orchestra

Disc 2

1. On The Sunny Side Of The Street (Fields/McHugh)
   Les Brown and His Band of Renown

2. Sentimental Journey (Green/Brown/Homer)
   Les Brown and His Band of Renown

3. September Song (Anderson/Weill)
   Douglas Gamley and His Orchestra

4. Smoke Gets In Your Eyes (Harbach/Kern)
   Marian McPartland, piano

5. Stormy Weather (Arlen/Koehler)
   Jo Stafford, vocal; Paul Weston and His Orchestra

6. Take The "A" Train (Strayhorn)
   Roland Shaw and His Orchestra

7. Tangerine (Mercer/Schertzinger)
   Peter Knight and His Orchestra

8. What Is This Thing Called Love? (Porter)
   Roland Shaw and His Orchestra

9. You Go To My Head (Gillespie/Coots)
   Harry James and His Orchestra

10. You Made Me Love You (McCarthy/Monaco)
    Les Brown and His Band of Renown

11. You'd Be So Nice To Come Home To (Porter)
    The Romantic Strings

N.B. *Please note that the musical arrangements included in this book may not exactly match the corresponding audio. Some songs were not included due to licensing restrictions.*

TABLE OF CONTENTS

N.B. *To avoid awkward page turns, the running order of this book differs slightly to that on the CDs.*

ABOUT THE SELECTIONS

The 20th century was full of history-making events—the Great Depression, landing on the moon, the invention of computers and the Internet—but none was more important or cataclysmic than World War II. The war and postwar period coincided with the decade of the 1940s, which musically saw the continuation of the big bands of the '30s and the emergence of solo singing stars. With millions of American fighting men and women being sent to Europe and Asia, the themes of separation and longing for home were prominent in our wartime songs. The music of the '40s played an important role in boosting American morale—both on the front lines and at home. It is not much of an exaggeration to say the great songs collected here helped win the war.

In addition to the wonderful arrangements in *Sentimental Journey*, the songbook contains two CDs with twenty-two recordings of the songs from Reader's Digest Music. A major player in the direct-mail sale of music for almost fifty years, Reader's Digest recorded hundreds of major artists, such as the late Jo Stafford, Harry James, Les Brown and other bandleaders. This introduction focuses on the songs on the CDs, since space unfortunately does not allow for discussion of all the songs.

Our title song, "Sentimental Journey," was one of the top hits of 1945 and the first million-seller for Les Brown and His Band of Renown. Brown wrote it with Ben Homer and Bud Green, and the young Doris Day became instantly famous for her vocal. The lyrics are about taking "that sentimental journey home"—a dream very much on the minds of millions of Americans in the spring of 1945 as the Allies were advancing on Berlin and the Japanese homeland. The recording heard here does not have Day's singing, but is by Les Brown and His Band of Renown from 1967, when he redid many of his hits exclusively for Reader's Digest. The smooth, gently swinging Brown sound is front and center on this version, which also benefits from the greatly improved recording technology of the '60s.

"As Time Goes By," probably the best-known movie song after "Over The Rainbow," first appeared in the 1931 stage review *Everybody's Welcome*. Rudy Vallee recorded it then, and it was a moderate hit. In 1942 it was featured throughout the soundtrack of *Casablanca*, the classic war romance starring Humphrey Bogart, Ingrid Bergman and Peter Lorre. Doolie Wilson sang it at the piano in Rick's Café Américaine after Bergman made her nostalgic request, "Play it, Sam." (She actually does not say, "Play it *again*, Sam," as many believe.) Because of a recording ban by the American Federation of Musicians at the time, Wilson was not able to release the song. Instead, RCA Victor reissued Vallee's earlier record, which went to No. 1. It is truly a treat to hear Jo

Stafford's version of "As Time Goes By" for Reader's Digest on the CDs. She became famous as a member of the Pied Pipers with Tommy Dorsey in the early '40s and went on to solo success on Capitol and Columbia Records. Stafford was known for her perfect pitch, though she herself discounted it. America lost one of the last great singers of the WWII era when she died in July 2008 at age 90.

Duke Ellington wrote "I'm Beginning To See The Light" with saxophonist Johnny Hodges, lyricist Don George and bandleader Harry James. It all began with Hodges doodling around with a "lick" during rehearsal. George liked it and added lyrics based on a song he heard in a movie about a revival meeting in the South. (One is reminded of Hank Williams' country classic "I Saw The Light.") The Harry James Orchestra released the first recording in January 1945, and it shot to No. 1. Ellington's came out shortly afterward and rose to No. 6. A few months later, Ella Fitzgerald and The Ink Spots' version racked up a No. 5 hit. Harry James reprises the song here in a late '60s recording for Reader's Digest with songbird Helen O'Connell on vocals. James and his band also do the romantic standard "You Go To My Head," a hit in 1938 for both bandleaders Larry Clinton and Glen Gray.

The movie musical *Cover Girl* was a big box-office hit in 1944, establishing Rita Hayworth as a GI pinup favorite. The songs, by Jerome Kern and Ira Gershwin, featured "Long Ago (And Far Away)," sung on the soundtrack by Nan Wynn dubbing for Hayworth. A slew of singers were quick to release recordings, with the duet by Helen O'Connell and Dick Haymes taking the laurels at No. 2. Bing Crosby, Jo Stafford and Perry Como also had Top Ten hits with the song that year. Singer-bandleader-arranger Alan Copeland and His Orchestra with Beverly Kelly on vocals perform it here on CD. Copeland was a member of the Modernaires from 1948 to 1952 and a regular on *The Bob Crosby Show* in the '50s.

The romantic standard "Moonglow" was written in 1934 by Will Hudson, Irving Mills and Eddie DeLange. The Dorsey Brothers Orchestra and Ethel Waters were the first to record it, but the top-selling records went to Benny Goodman and Duke Ellington that year. The song continued to be popular during the WWII years and the '50s. In 1955 Columbia Pictures staff composer George Duning melded his *Picnic* theme together with "Moonglow," and Morris Stoloff and the Columbia Pictures Orchestra's recording hit No. 1. Forty years later Tony Bennett sang "Moonglow" with k.d. lang on his *MTV Unplugged* CD. It went platinum, became his best-selling album ever with more than a million sold and won him the prestigious Album of the Year GRAMMY® Award. Les Brown's late '60s instrumental version for Reader's Digest is included on the CD.

The WWII popularity of "You Made Me Love You (I Didn't Want To Do It)" is mainly owing to Harry James. Al Jolson introduced it in 1913, and it was his fourth No. 1 smash since arriving on Broadway in 1911. By the early '40s, of course, it was a well-worn standard, but James gave "You Made Me Love You" a big-band makeover that propelled it to the Top Five and was his first million-seller. Les Brown's recording on the CD is again a late '60s track for Reader's Digest.

Duke Ellington is considered by some to be the single most creative talent in American musical history. By the beginning of WWII, he was a major force in jazz and swing with over fifty chart hits. In 1941 he released "Take The 'A' Train," his signature theme referring to the New York City subway line, written by close friend Billy Strayhorn. Although it is one of the most recognizable swing themes, the song made it to only No. 11 on the charts. Two years later it reappeared as a hit when Ellington performed it in the film *Reveille with Betty,* starring Ann Miller as a disc jockey doing a show for the troops. The thin plot was basically an excuse to parade big names like Ellington, Frank Sinatra and Count Basie.

A collection like this would not be complete without a few "torch songs," and here we have two of the best: "Smoke Gets In Your Eyes" and "Stormy Weather." Singer-actress Tamara introduced the Jerome Kern-Otto Harbach classic "Smoke Gets In Your Eyes" in the 1933 musical *Roberta.* Various artists, including torch singer extraordinaire Ruth Etting, had big hits with it at the time, and during the war years it was Artie Shaw's version with the Gramercy Five that ruled the roost. Of course, the biggest revival of all was the Platter's classic 1959 hit with Tony Williams on lead vocal. Noted jazz pianist Marian McPartland, who for years had a jazz show on National Public Radio, performs it here on CD.

"Stormy Weather," penned by Harold Arlen and Ted Koehler, made its debut in 1933 with a recording by Leo Reisman's Orchestra with Arlen himself on vocals. It was a No. 1 hit, as was another recording by Ethel Waters the same year. However, ten years later a version by Lena Horne, from the film of the same name in which she starred, made such an impression that she is forever identified with the song. The 1943 movie musical *Stormy Weather* was the greatest onscreen showcase of African American talent up to its time. Jo Stafford gives an appropriately bluesy rendition on the CD.

"All Or Nothing At All," the opening track on CD 1, was Frank Sinatra's first No. 1 million-seller as a solo artist in 1943. Previously, he was the featured "boy singer" for Harry James and Tommy Dorsey, before going out on his own in 1942. The recording of "All Or Nothing At All" actually was a re-release of one he made with Harry James's band in 1939—only this time Sinatra got top billing on the disc label instead of James.

The novelty song "Mairzy Doats And Dozy Doats" was written by songwriters Milton Drake, Alan Hoffman and Jerry Livingston. Drake recalled that the idea came to him when his young daughter sang an English nursery rhyme that starts "Cowzy tweet and sowzy tweet and liddle sharksy doisters." The songwriting team transformed that into "Mairzy doats and dozy doats and liddle lamzy divey" ("Mares eat oats and does eat oats and little lambs eat ivy"). In 1944 the Merry Macs had a No. 1 hit with the tune, and it is said that U.S. troops in WWII used phrases from the lyrics as passwords.

"It's Only A Paper Moon" juxtaposes a make-believe "Barnum and Bailey world" with the reality of true love. The lyrics came from outstanding lyricist E.Y. Harburg ("Over The Rainbow") and Broadway producer Billy Rose, with music by Harold Arlen. It appeared in 1933 in an unsuccessful play, *The Great Magoo,* and also in the film *Take a Chance.* But the song's lasting fame is owing to hit recordings in 1945 by Ella Fitzgerald and Benny Goodman, as well as the King Cole Trio. In 1973 it provided the title to the Peter Bogdanovich film *Paper Moon,* starring Ryan and Tatum O'Neal.

Trumpeter Billy Butterfield, who played with Artie Shaw, Benny Goodman and Les Brown, established his own orchestra and began recording on the fledgling Capitol label in 1943. Two years later he released "Moonlight In Vermont" with Margaret Whiting on vocals, and it turned into a million-seller and his biggest hit ever. After the war, Whiting became a solo artist for Capitol and in 1954 did a new version of "Moonlight In Vermont" that was a hit all over again.

In the pre-Elvis era, American popular music was blessed with an abundance of well-crafted songs that have entered the canon of the "Great American Songbook." All of the songs in *Sentimental Journey* have stood the test of time and earned a place in that canon. Perhaps what is more important is that they did much to keep hope alive during the greatest conflict in world history.

— **Rick Hessney**

All I Do Is Dream Of You

Words by Arthur Freed
Music by Nacio Herb Brown

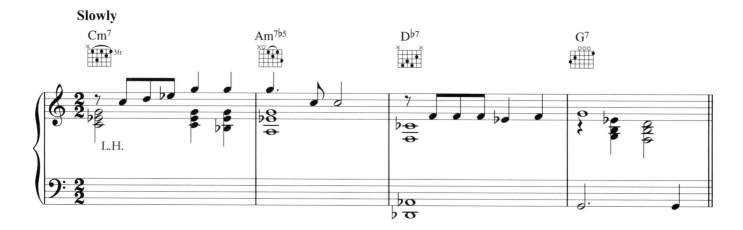

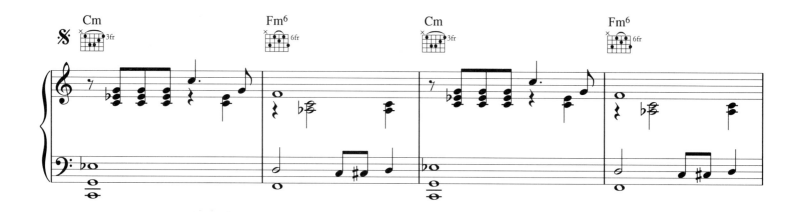

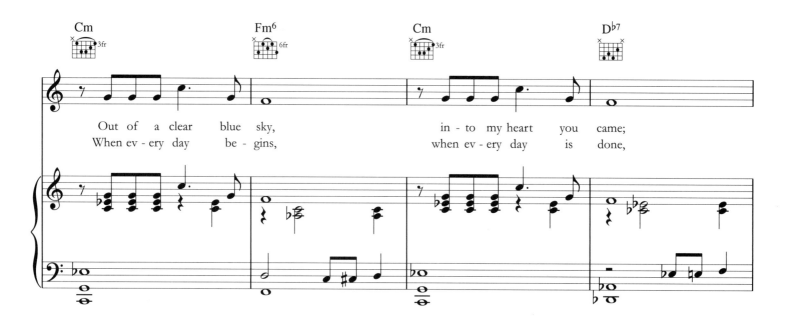

Out of a clear blue sky, into my heart you came;
When ev-ery day be-gins, when ev-ery day is done,

not for a day,   but here to stay;   I'll al-ways feel   the   same.
here in my heart,   ne - ver to part,   you'll al-ways be   the   one.

Brightly

All I do is dream of you the whole night through,_____

with the dawn, I still go on and dream of you._____ You're

every thought, you're every-thing, you're every song I ever sing;

Sum - mer, Win - ter, Au - tumn and Spring, and

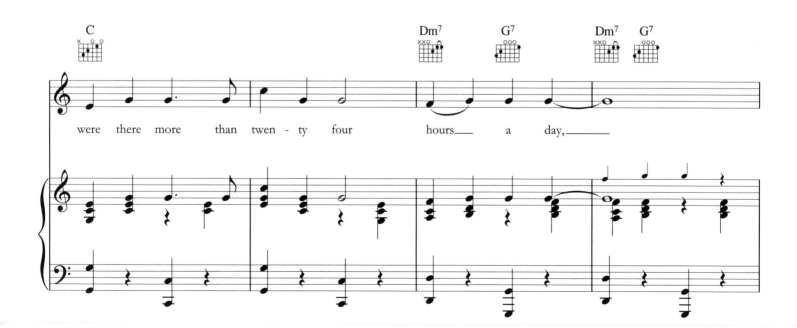

were there more than twen - ty four hours___ a day,___

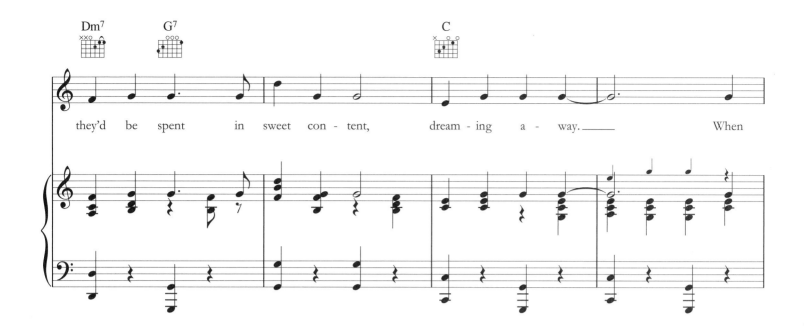

they'd be spent in sweet con - tent, dream - ing a - way._____ When

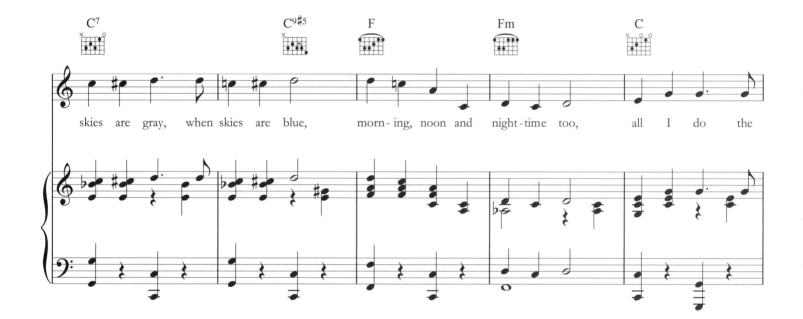

skies are gray, when skies are blue, morn - ing, noon and night - time too, all I do the

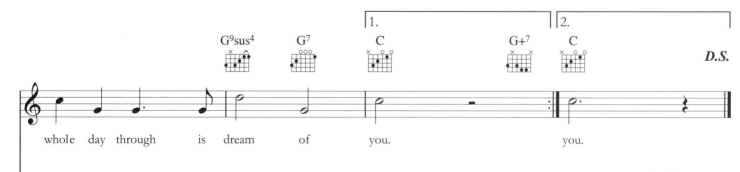

whole day through is dream of you. you.

All Or Nothing At All

Words by Jack Lawrence

Music by Arthur Altman

Moderately slow *(with much expression)*

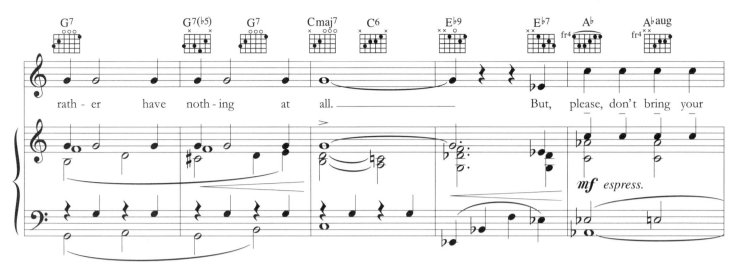

rath-er have noth-ing at all. _____ But, please, don't bring your

lips so close to my cheek. _____ Don't smile or I'll be lost be-yond re-

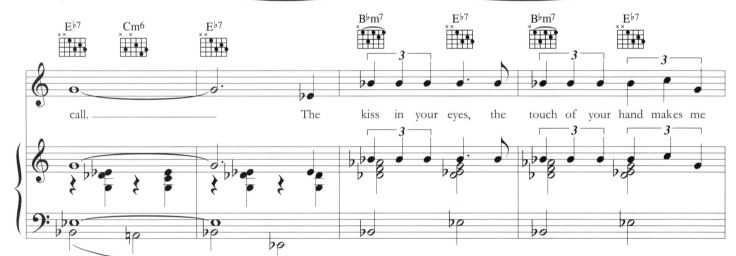

call. _____ The kiss in your eyes, the touch of your hand makes me

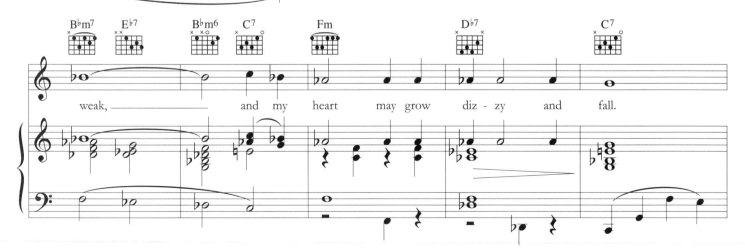

weak, _____ and my heart may grow diz-zy and fall.

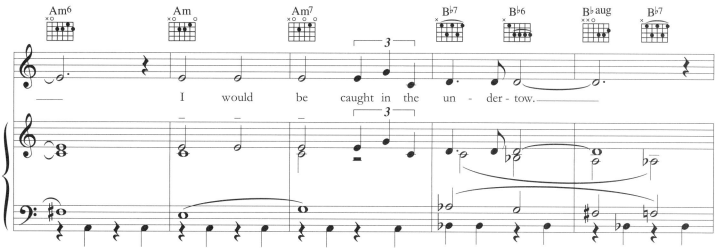

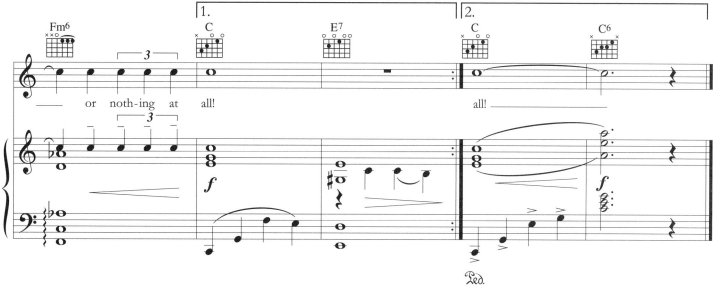

As Time Goes By
Words and Music by Herman Hupfield

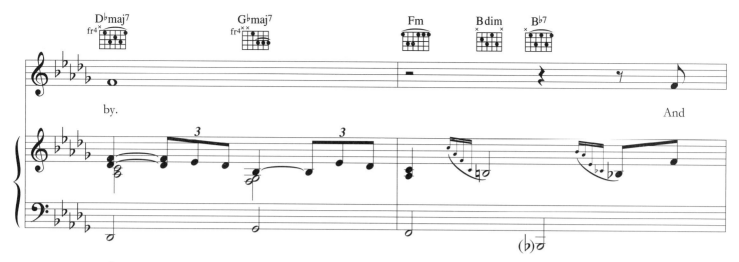

by.   And

when two lov-ers woo, they still say "I love you," on

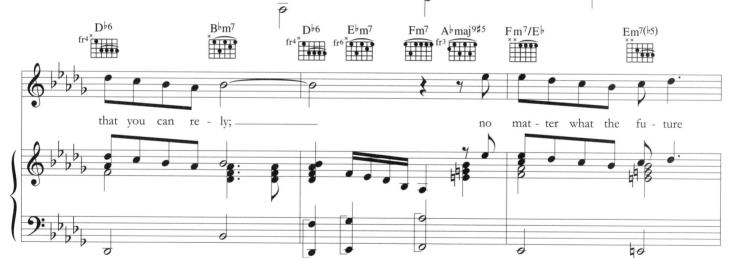

that you can re-ly; _____ no mat-ter what the fu-ture

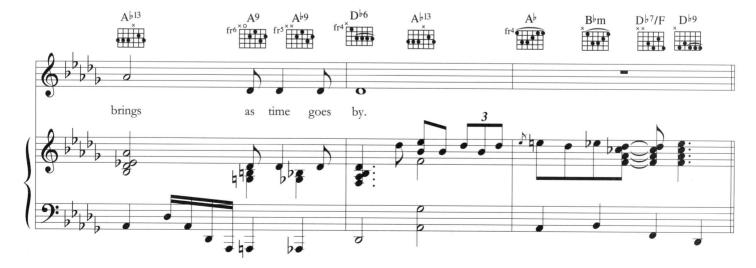

brings as time goes by.

world will al-ways wel-come lov-ers as time goes by.

by.

Dream

Words and Music by Johnny Mercer

Get in touch with that sun - down fel - low____ as he tip - toes a - cross the

sand. He's got a mil - lion kinds of star - dust, pick your fav - 'rite

brand, and dream,_____ when you're feel - in' blue,_____

dream,_____ that's the thing to do,_____ just_____ watch the smoke rings

rise in the air,___ you'll find your share___ of me - mor - ies there.___ So

dream, _____ when the day is through, _____ dream, _____ and they might come

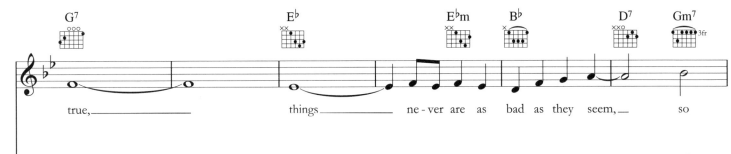

true, _____ things _____ ne - ver are as bad as they seem, _ so

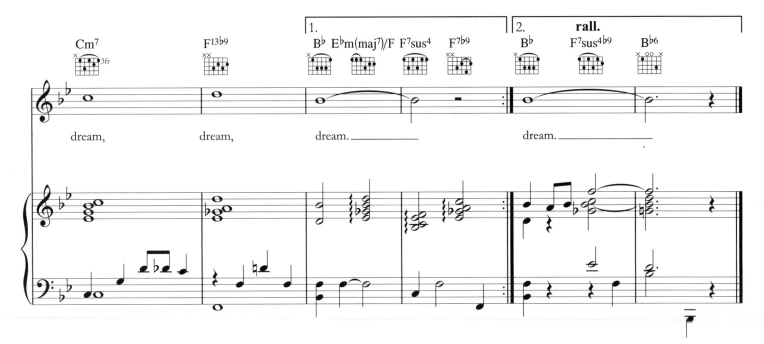

dream, dream, dream. _____ dream.

I'll Walk Alone

Lyric by Sammy Cahn

Music by Jule Styne

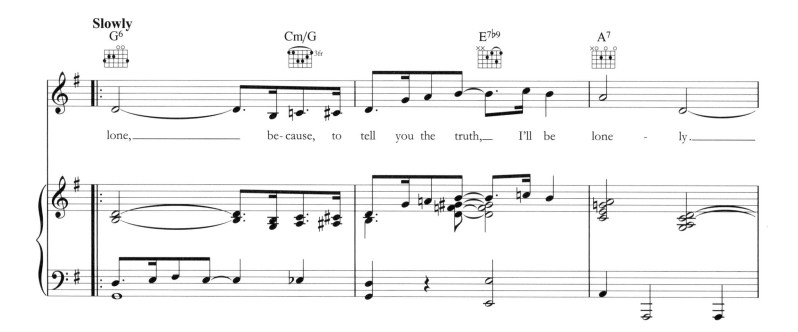

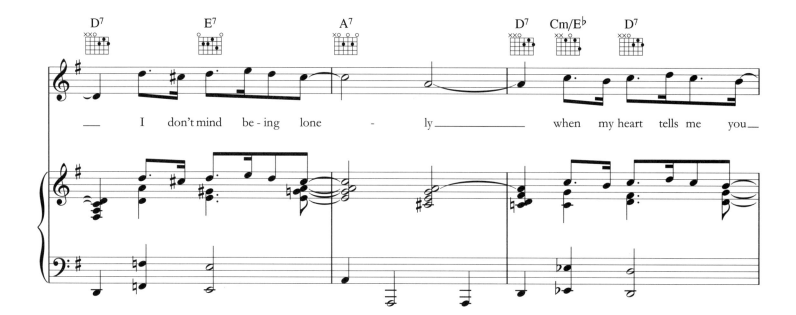

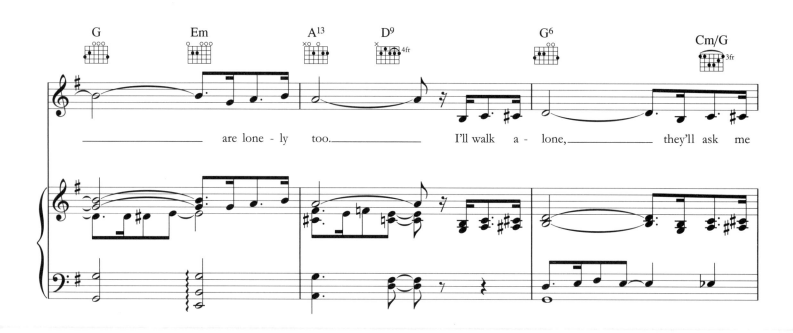

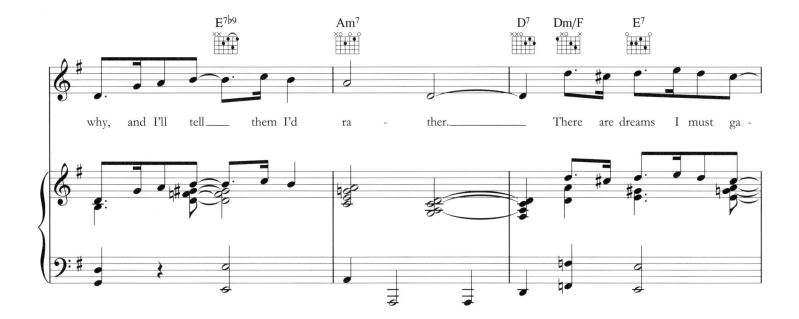

why, and I'll tell____ them I'd ra - ther._____ There are dreams I must ga -

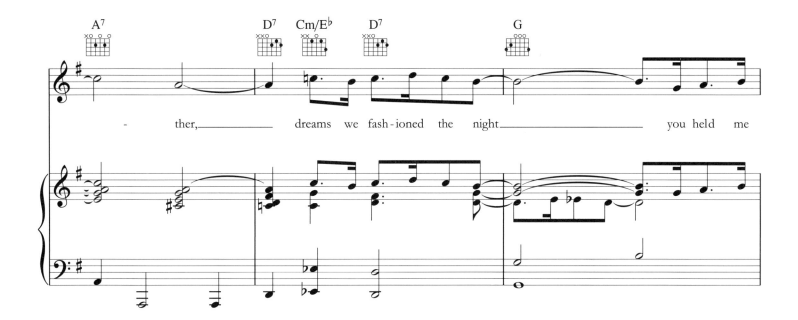

- ther,_____ dreams we fash-ioned the night_____ you held me

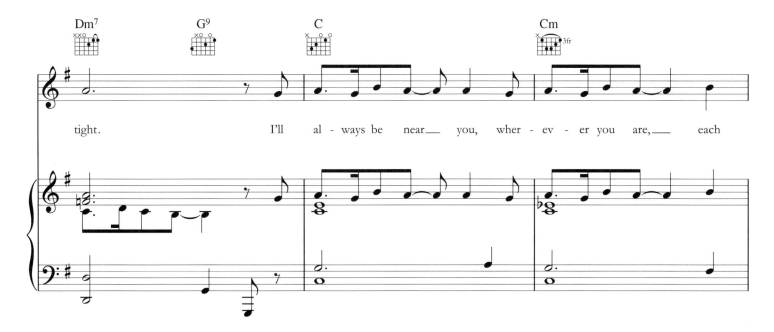

tight. I'll al - ways be near____ you, wher - ev - er you are,____ each

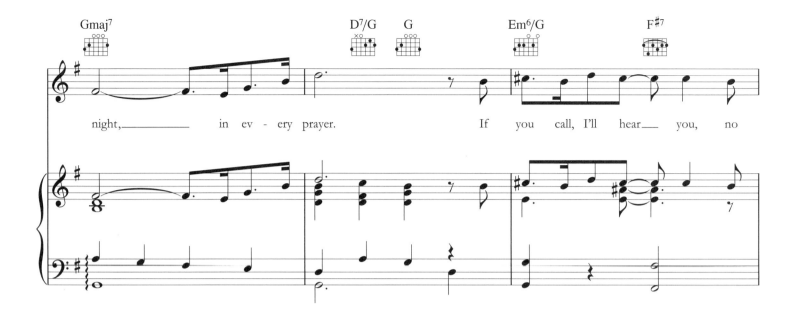

night,_____ in ev - ery prayer. If you call, I'll hear___ you, no

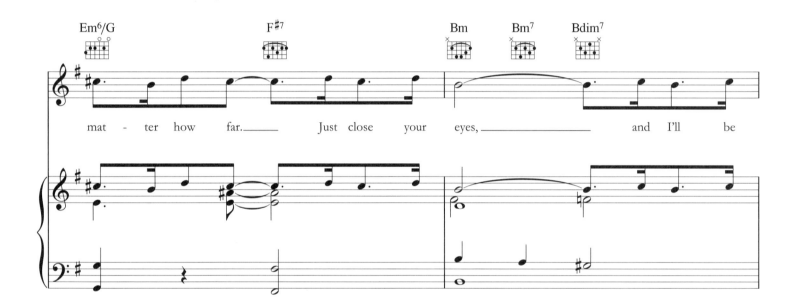

mat - ter how far._____ Just close your eyes,_____ and I'll be

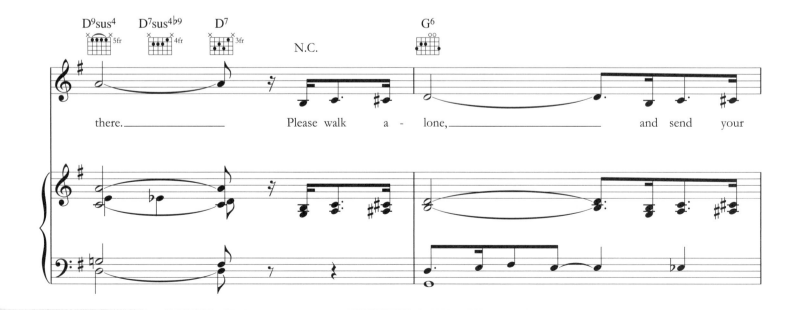

there._____ Please walk a - lone,_____ and send your

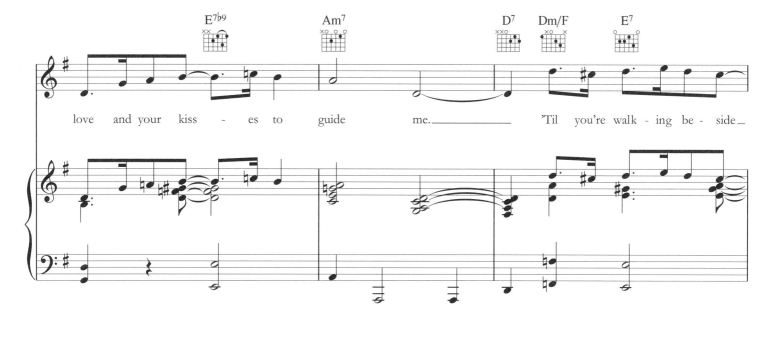

love and your kiss - es to guide me._____ 'Til you're walk - ing be - side__

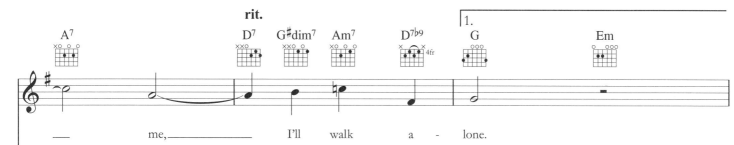

_____ me,_____ I'll walk a - lone.

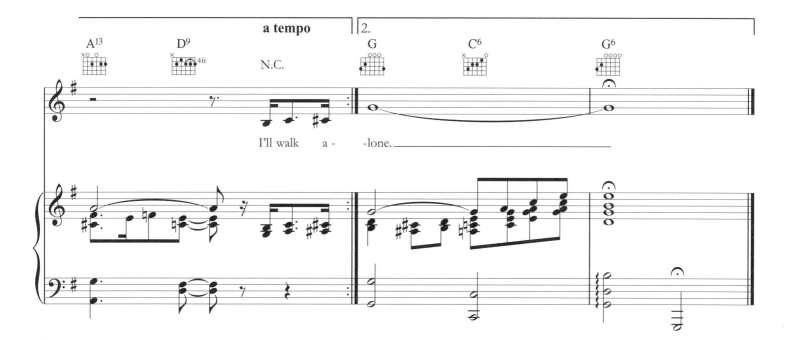

I'll walk a - -lone._____

I Can't Begin To Tell You

Words by Mack Gordon
Music by James V. Monaco

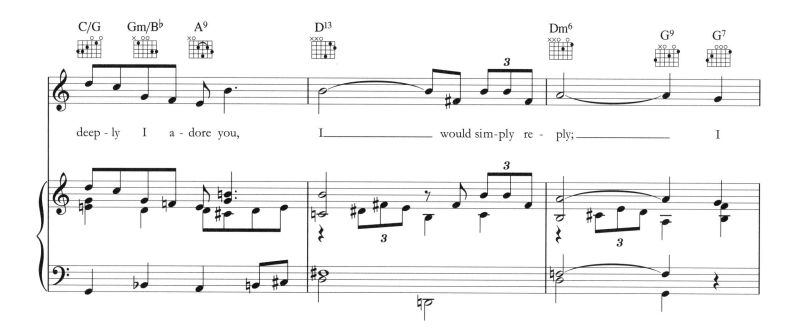

deep - ly I a - dore you, I _____ would sim-ply re - ply; _____ I

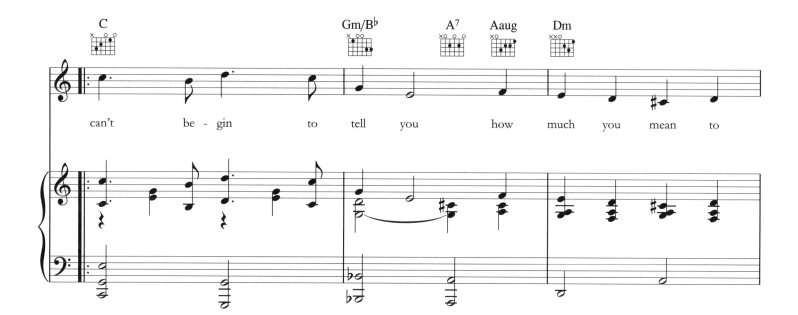

can't be - gin to tell you how much you mean to

me, my world would end if ev - er we were

through._____ I can't be-gin to tell you how hap-py I would

be, if I could speak my mind like oth-ers do._____

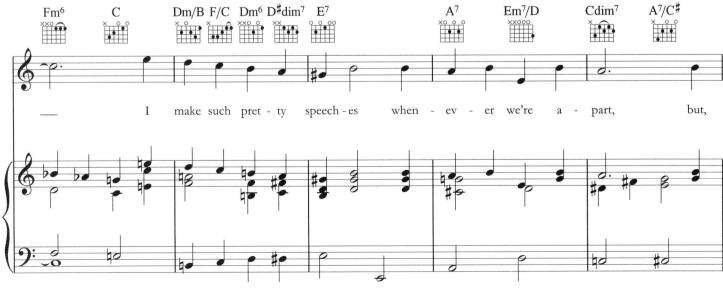

__ I make such pret-ty speech-es when-ev-er we're a-part, but,

when you're near,_ the words I choose_ re-fuse to leave my heart. So,

take the sweet-est phras-es the world has ev-er known, and make be-lieve I've

said them all_ to you._ I you._

I Love You
Words and Music by Cole Porter

night_____ till you'd re-lent and con-sent to be mine_____

____ but a-las, just an am-a-teur am I_____

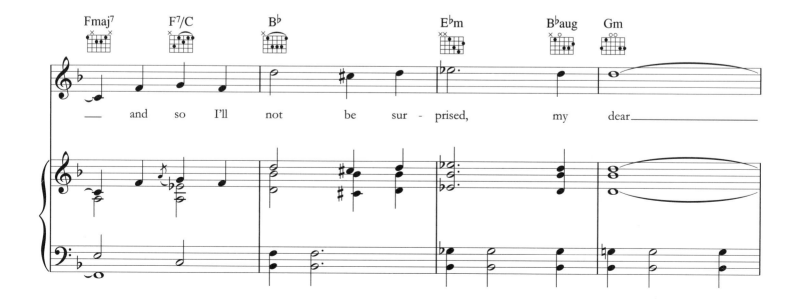

____ and so I'll not be sur-prised, my dear_____

if you smile and po - lite - ly pass it by_____

___ when this, my first___ love song, you hear. "I

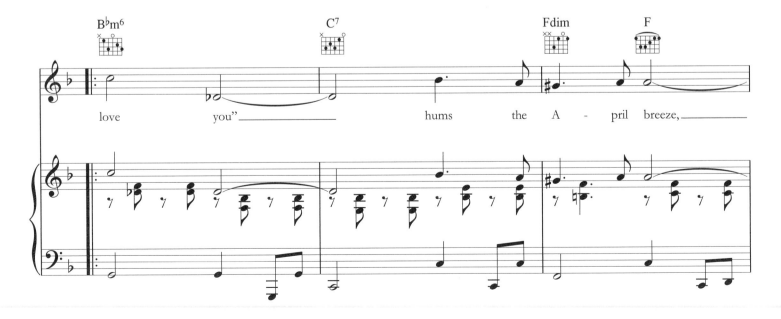

love you"_____ hums the A - pril breeze,_____

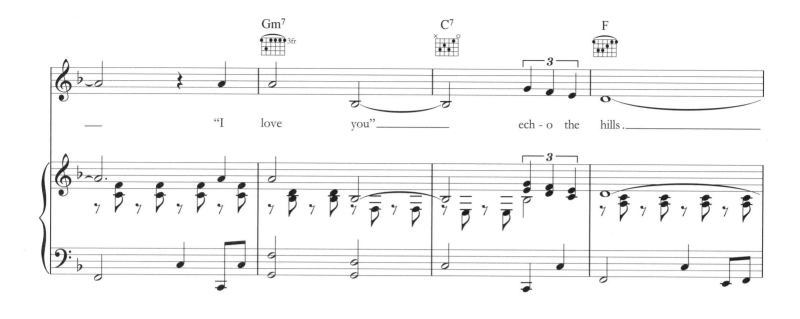

It's spring a-gain _____ and birds on the wing a-gain _____

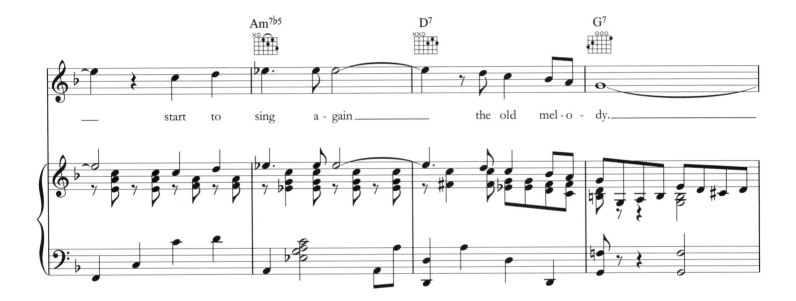

_____ start to sing a-gain _____ the old mel-o-dy. _____

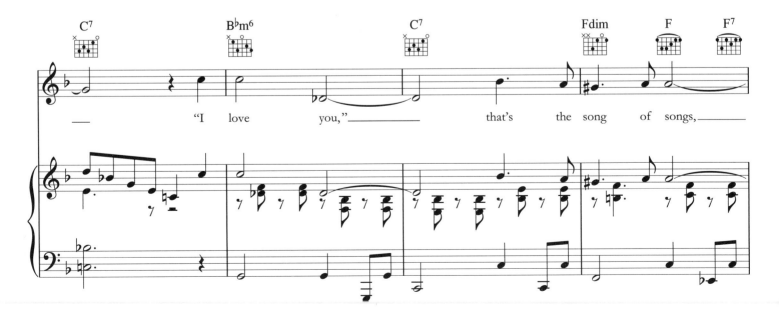

_____ "I love you," _____ that's the song of songs, _____

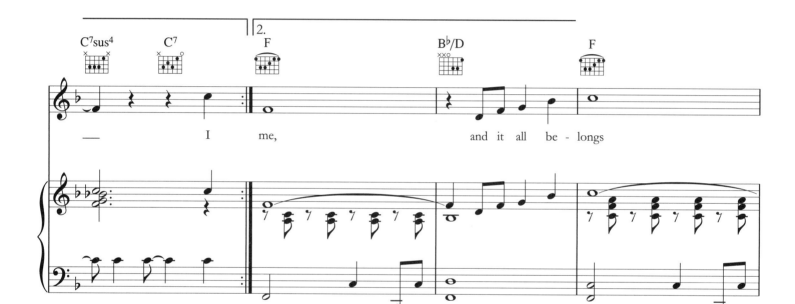

I'm Beginning To See The Light

Words and Music by Don George, Johnny Hodges, Duke Ellington and Harry James

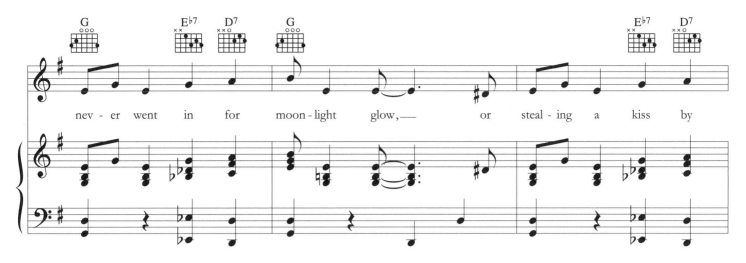

never went in for moon-light glow,— or steal-ing a kiss by

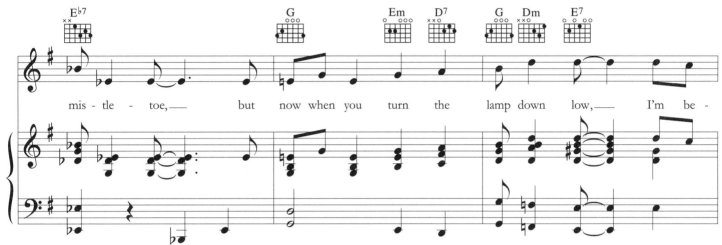

mis-tle-toe,— but now when you turn the lamp down low,— I'm be-

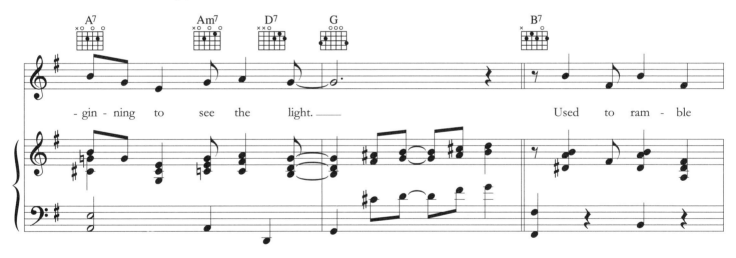

-gin-ning to see the light.— Used to ram-ble

through the park,— all a-lone there in the dark,—

then you came and caused a spark, — and my heart is on fire — now, —

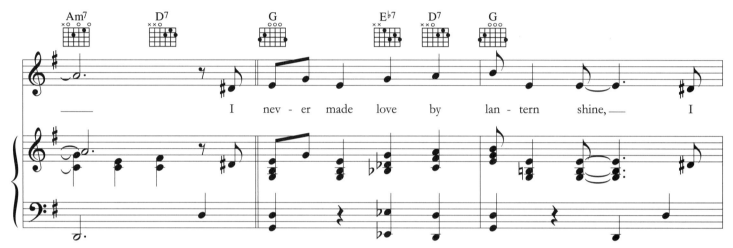

— I nev-er made love by lan-tern shine, — I

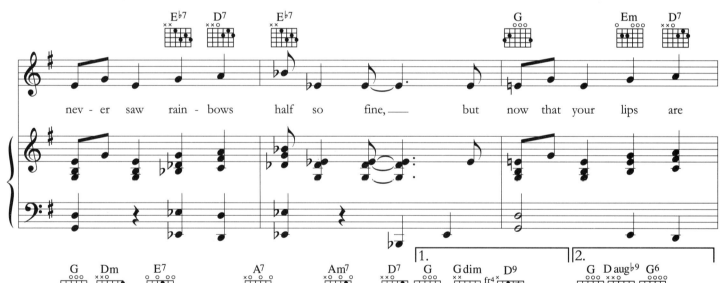

nev-er saw rain-bows half so fine, — but now that your lips are

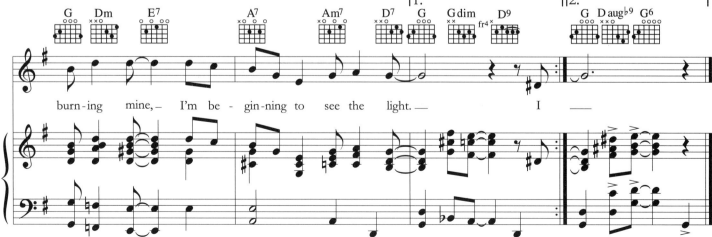

burn-ing mine, — I'm be-gin-ning to see the light. — I —

It's Only A Paper Moon

Music by Harold Arlen

Lyrics by E.Y. Harburg and Billy Rose

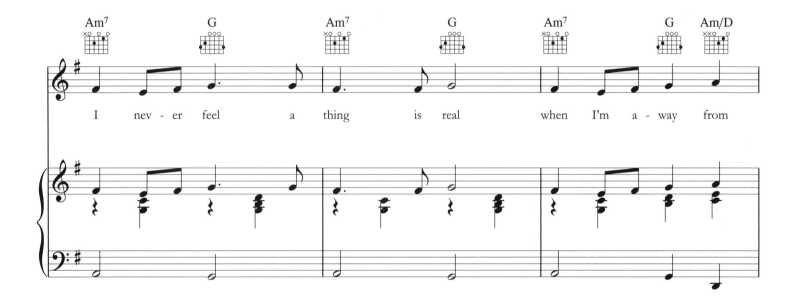

I nev-er feel a thing is real when I'm a-way from

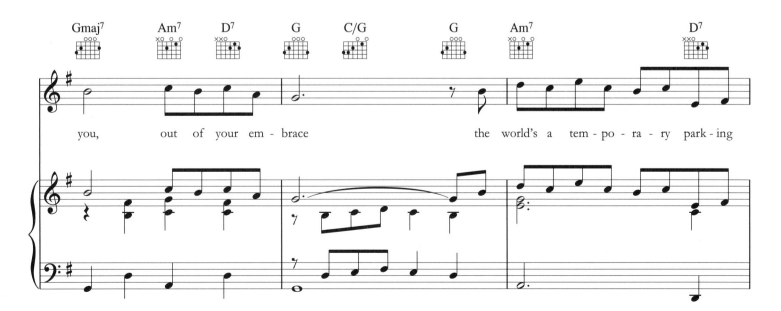

you, out of your em-brace the world's a tem-po-ra-ry park-ing

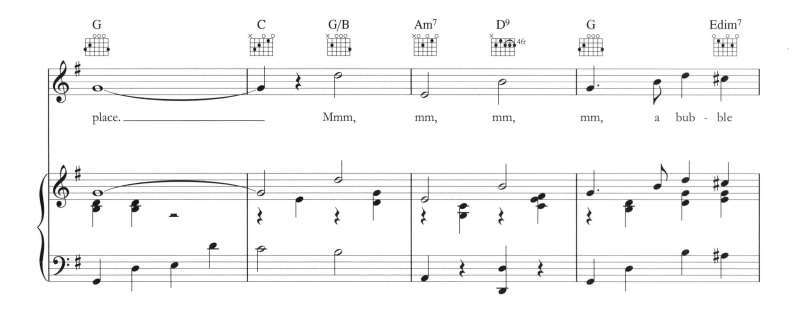

place. _____ Mmm, mm, mm, mm, a bub - ble

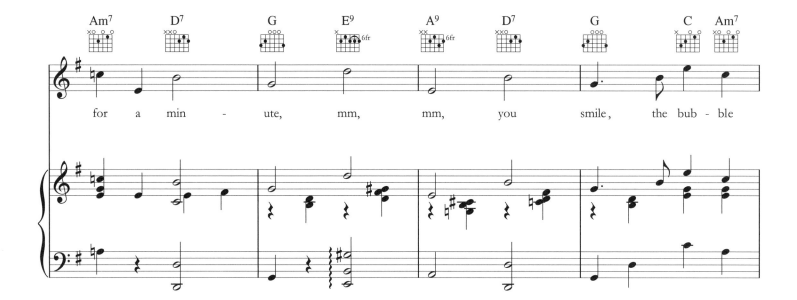

for a min - ute, mm, mm, you smile, the bub - ble

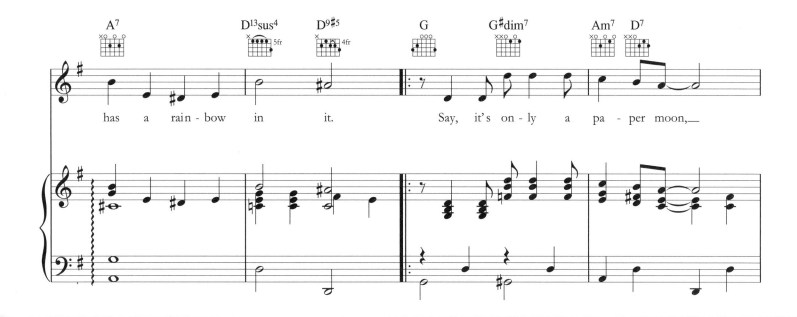

has a rain-bow in it. Say, it's on-ly a pa - per moon,___

sail - ing ov - er a card-board sea, ___ but it would-n't be make - be - lieve, ___ if you ___

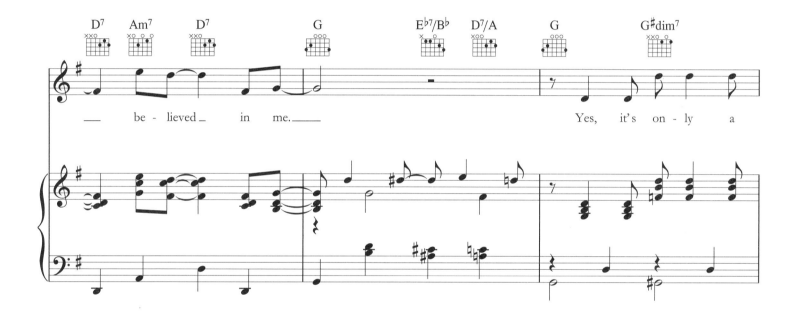

___ be - lieved ___ in me. ___ Yes, it's on - ly a

can - vas sky, ___ hang - ing ov - er a mus - lin tree, ___

but it would-n't be make-be-lieve_ if you_ be-lieved_ in me._

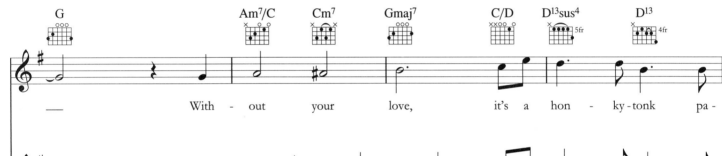

_ With-out your love, it's a hon-ky-tonk pa-

rade, with-out your love, it's a

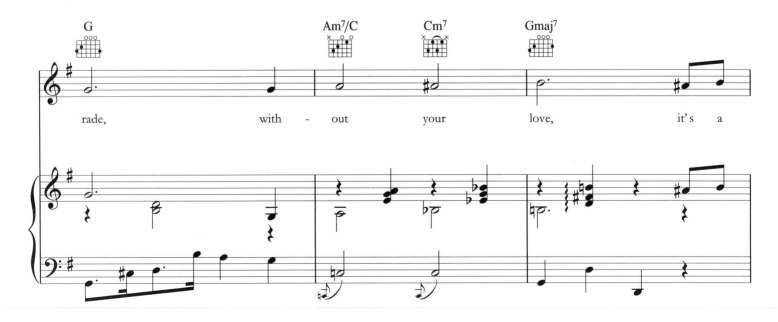

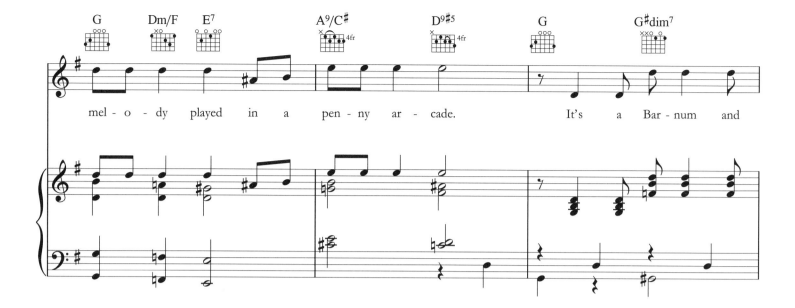

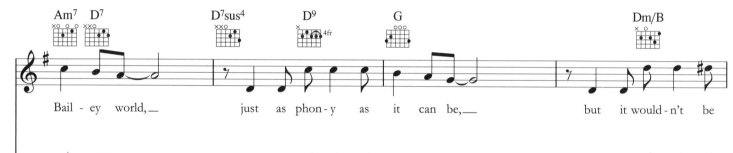

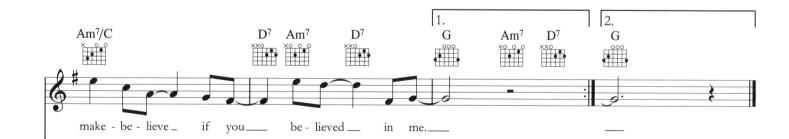

It's Magic

Words by Sammy Cahn
Music by Jule Styne

props;   things I used to think were in-con-ceiv-a-ble,

you've a way of mak-ing them be-liev-a-ble   and up-on a night   like

this   I'm a-fraid you just   can't   miss.

You sigh, the song be-gins, you speak and I hear vi-o-lins, it's

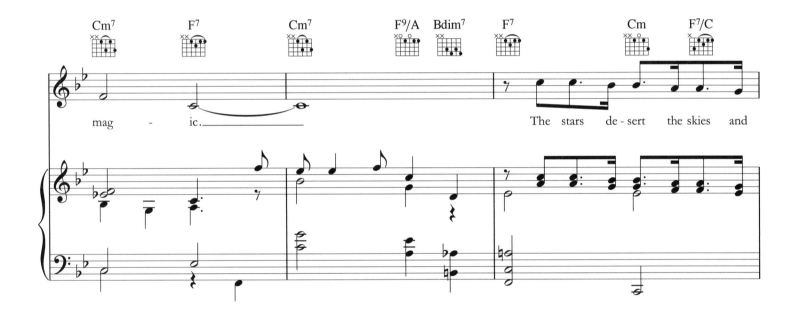

mag - ic._____ The stars de-sert the skies and

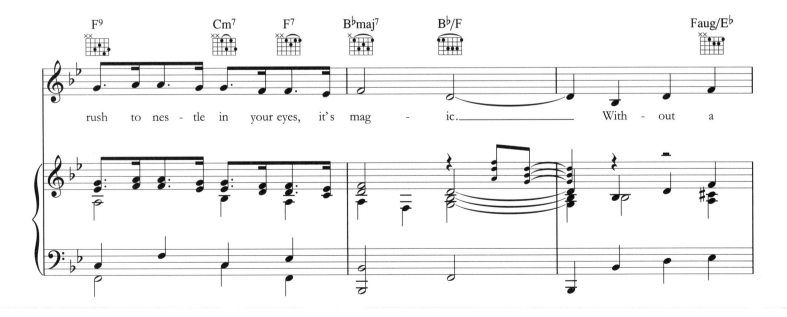

rush to nes-tle in your eyes, it's mag - ic._____ With-out a

gold - en wand_____ or mys - tic charms,_____

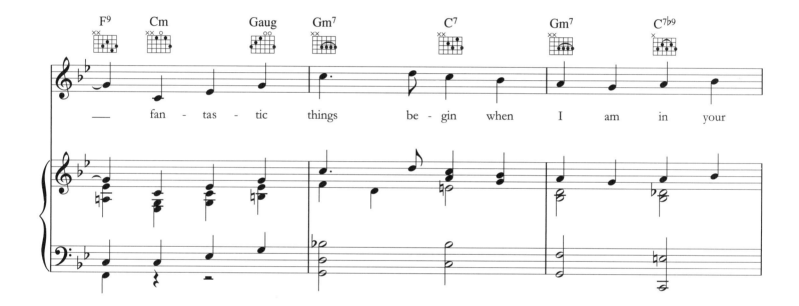

— fan - tas - tic things be - gin when I am in your

arms._____ When we walk hand in hand the

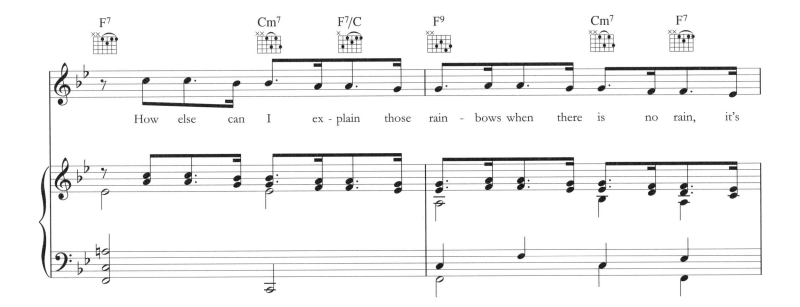

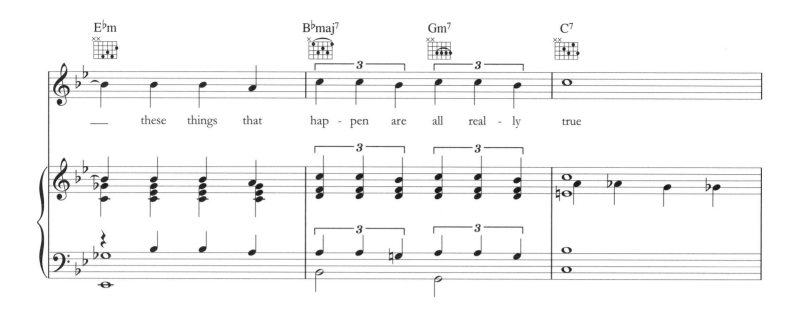

these things that hap - pen are all real - ly true

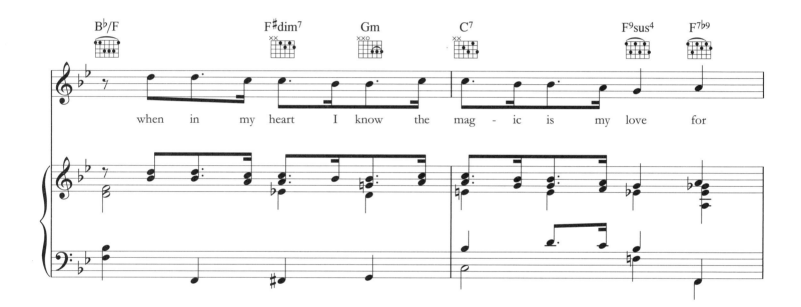

when in my heart I know the mag - ic is my love for

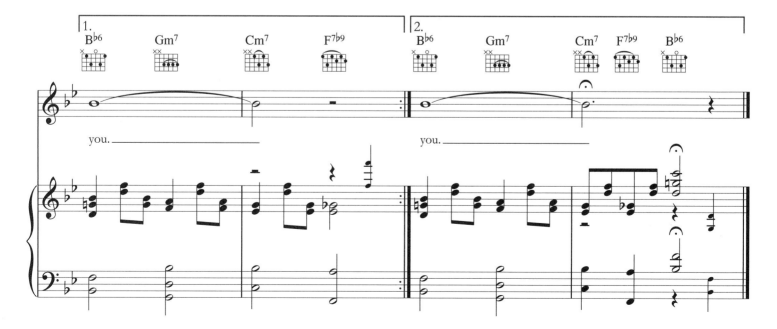

you. _____   you. _____

Let's Fall In Love

By Ted Koehler and Harold Arlen

I have a feel-ing, it's a feel-ing I'm con-ceal-ing, I don't know why.

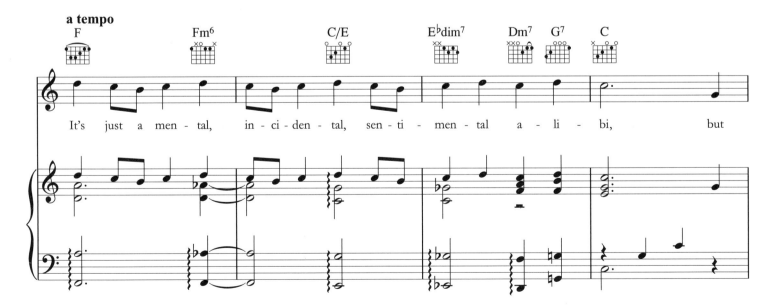

It's just a men-tal, in-ci-den-tal, sen-ti-men-tal a-li-bi, but

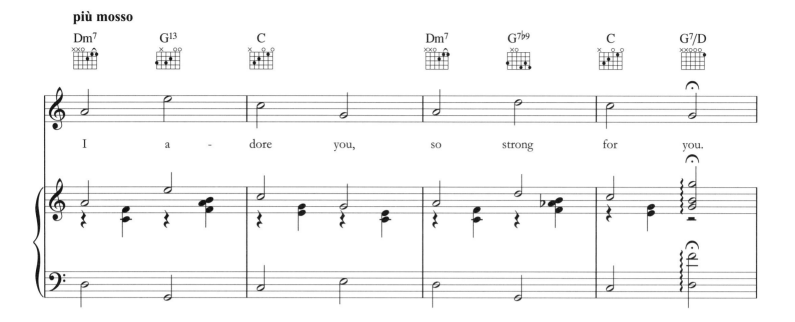

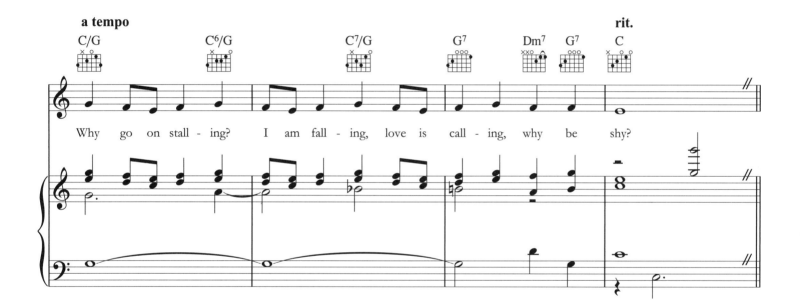

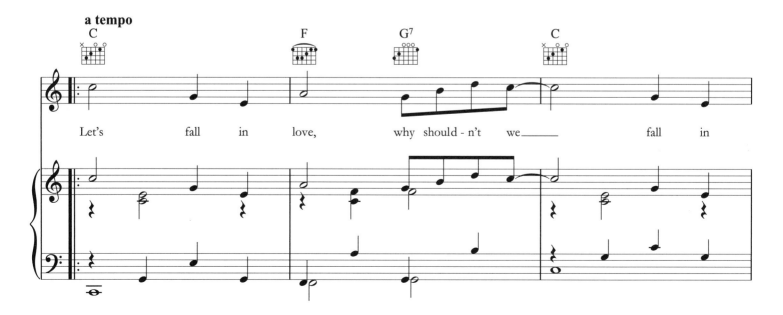

love? Our hearts are made___ of it, let's take a chance,___ why be a-fraid___

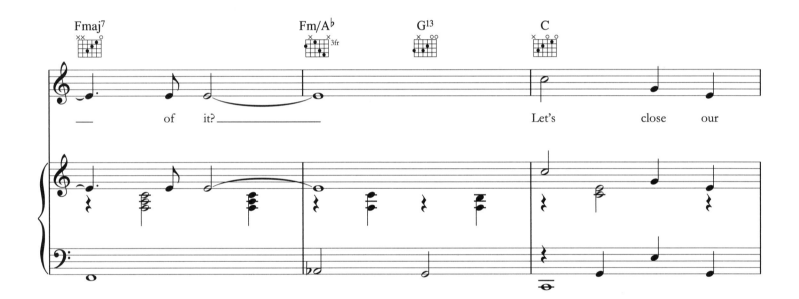

___ of it?_____ Let's close our

eyes, and make our own___ pa - ra - dise. Lit - tle we know___

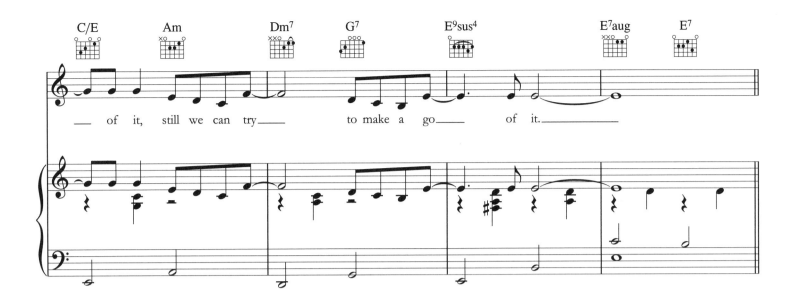

_of it, still we can try_____ to make a go____ of it._____

più mosso

We might have been meant for each oth - er,_____ to

rit.

be or not to be, let our hearts dis - cov - er.

Let's fall in love, why should-n't we____ fall in love? Now is the time_

____ for it while we are young, let's fall in love.____

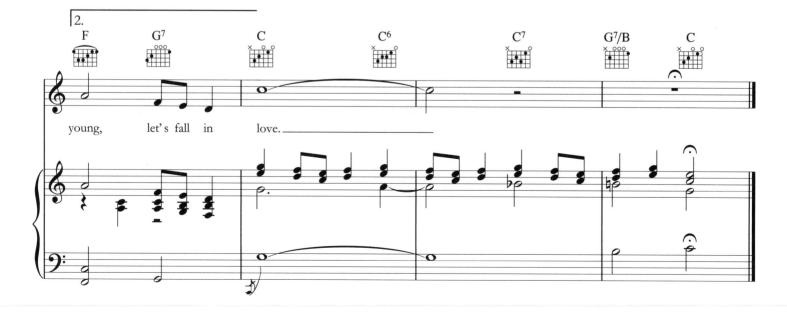

young, let's fall in love.____

Moonlight In Vermont

By Karl Suessdorf and John Blackburn

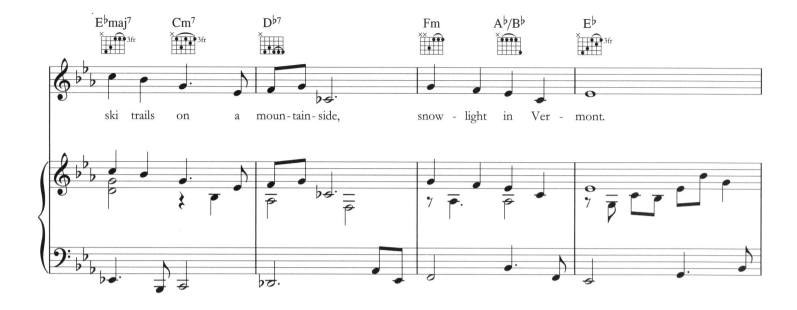

ski trails on a moun-tain-side, snow-light in Ver-mont.

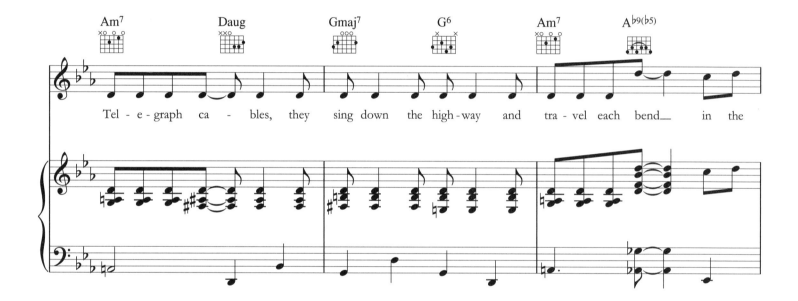

Tel - e - graph ca - bles, they sing down the high-way and tra-vel each bend___ in the

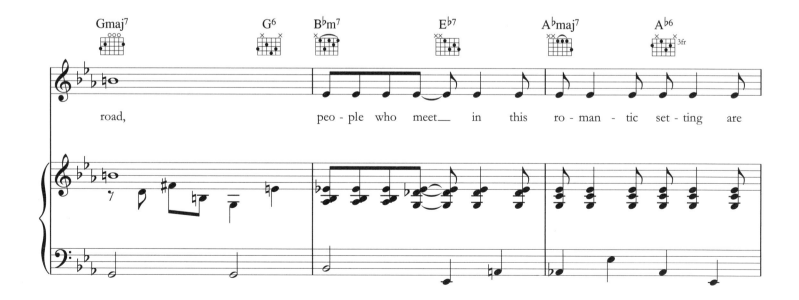

road, peo - ple who meet___ in this ro - man - tic set - ting are

so hyp-no-tized_ by the love - ly ev -'ning sum - mer breeze.

Warb-ling of a mea-dow-lark, moon-light in Ver - mont.

You and I and moon-light in Ver - mont. -mont.

Long Ago (And Far Away)

(from *COVER GIRL*)

Words by Ira Gershwin

Music by Jerome Kern

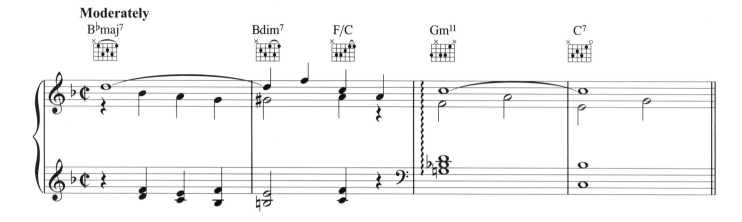

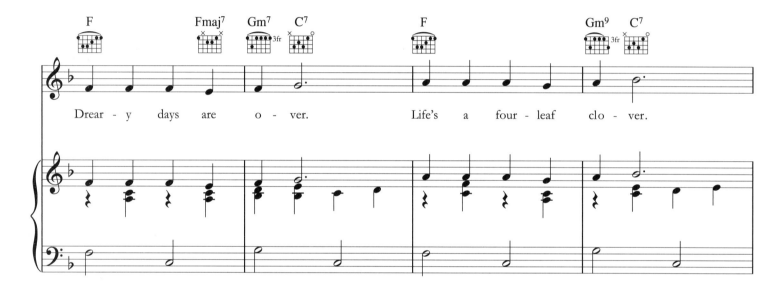

Drear - y days are o - ver. Life's a four - leaf clo - ver.

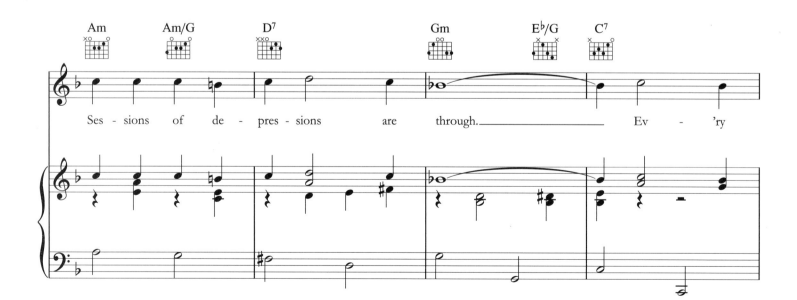

Ses - sions of de - pres - sions are through. _____ Ev - 'ry

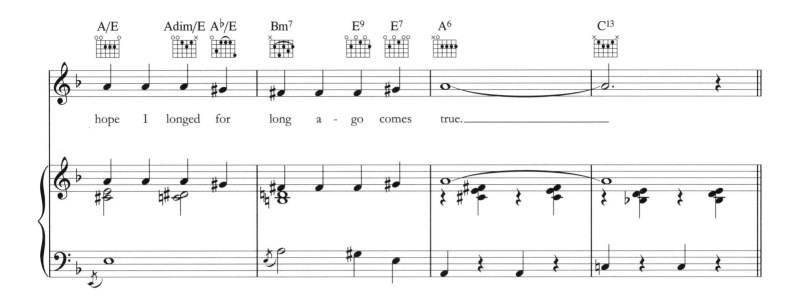

hope I longed for long a - go comes true._____

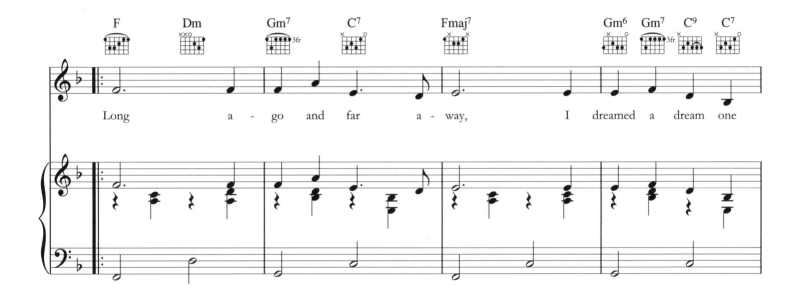

Long a - go and far a - way, I dreamed a dream one

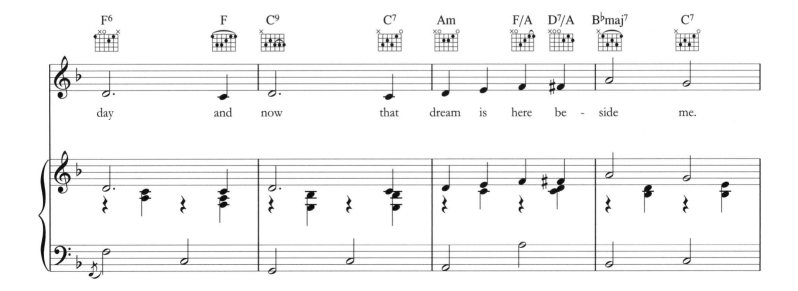

day and now that dream is here be - side me.

59

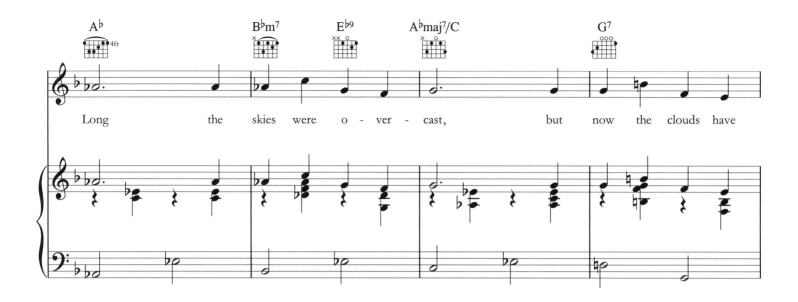

Long the skies were o‑ver‑cast, but now the clouds have

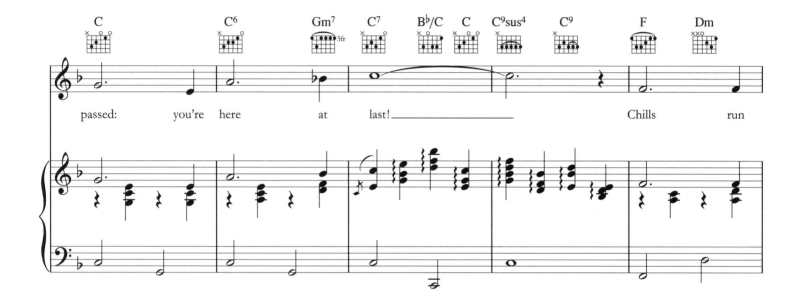

passed: you're here at last! _____ Chills run

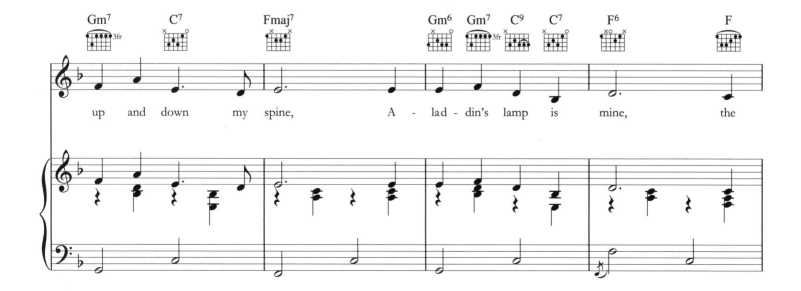

up and down my spine, A‑lad‑din's lamp is mine, the

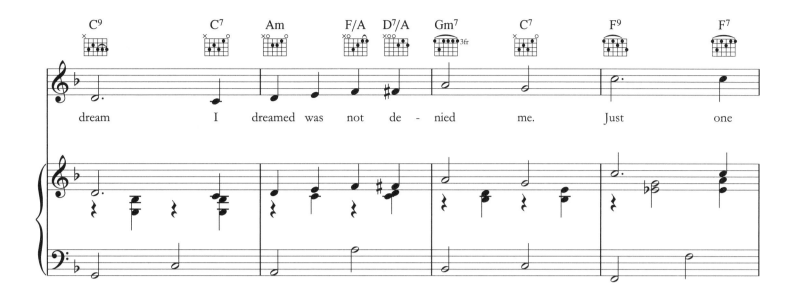

dream   I   dreamed   was   not   de - nied   me.   Just   one

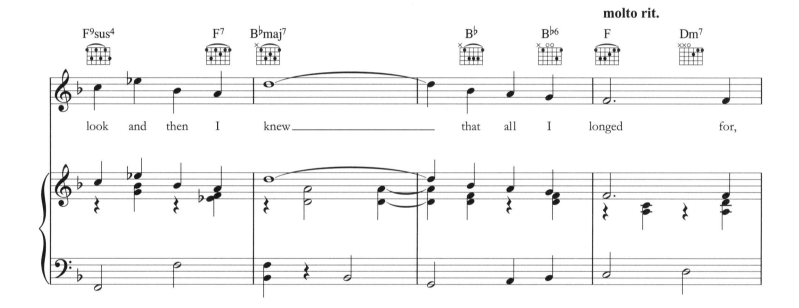

molto rit.

look   and   then   I   knew _____ that   all   I   longed   for,

a tempo

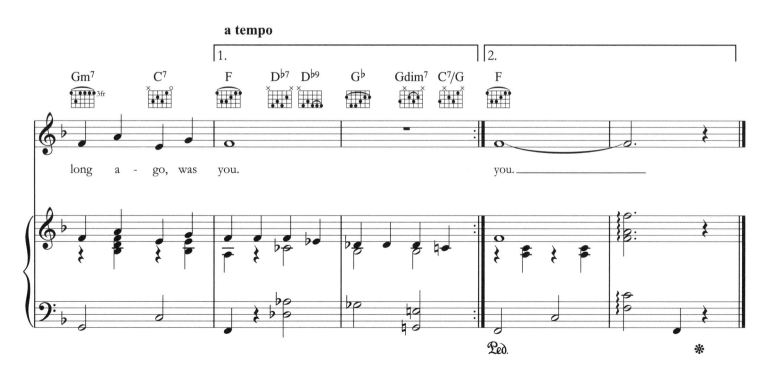

long   a - go,   was   you.   you. _____

Mairzy Doats And Dozy Doats

Words and Music by Al Hoffman, Milton Drake and Jerry Livingston

Moderately, with humor

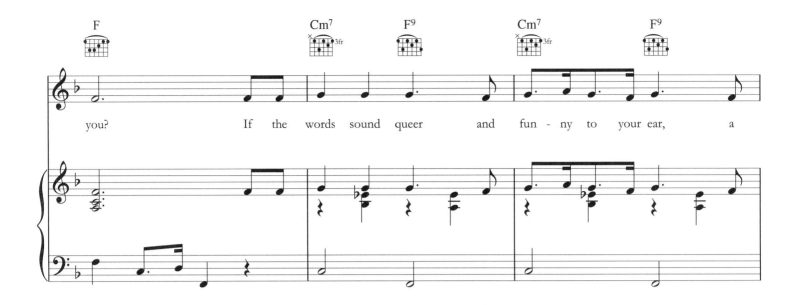

you? If the words sound queer and fun-ny to your ear, a

lit-tle bit jum-bled and jiv-ey, sing, "Mares eat oats and

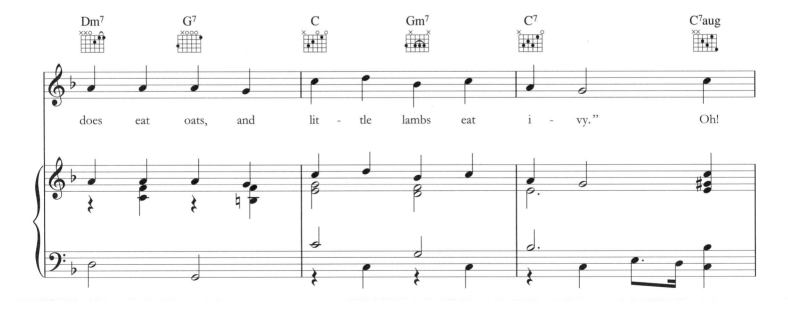

does eat oats, and lit-tle lambs eat i-vy." Oh!

Mair - zy doats and do - zy doats and lid - dle lam - zy div - ey, a

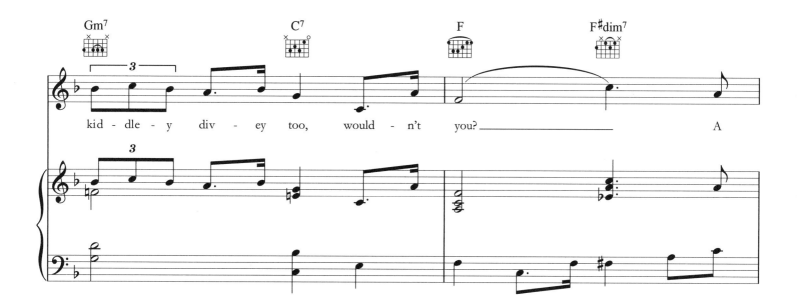

kid - dle - y div - ey too, would - n't you? _____ A

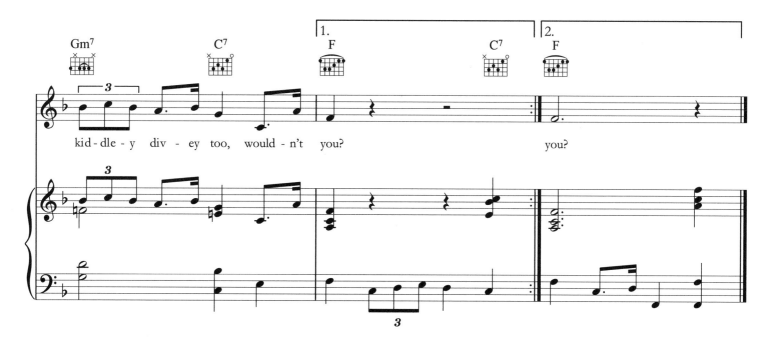

kid - dle - y div - ey too, would - n't you?   you?

65

Moonglow

Words and Music by Will Hudson, Eddie De Lange and Irving Mills

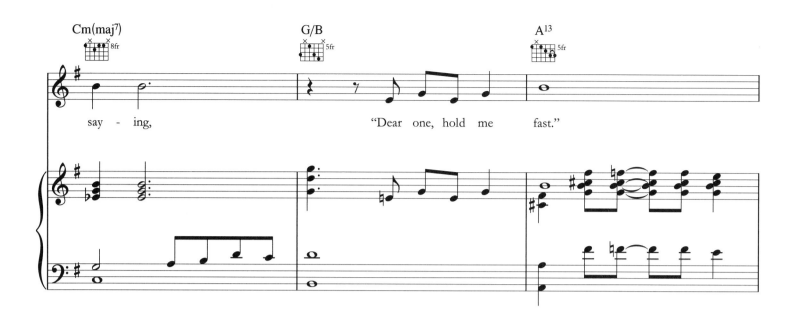

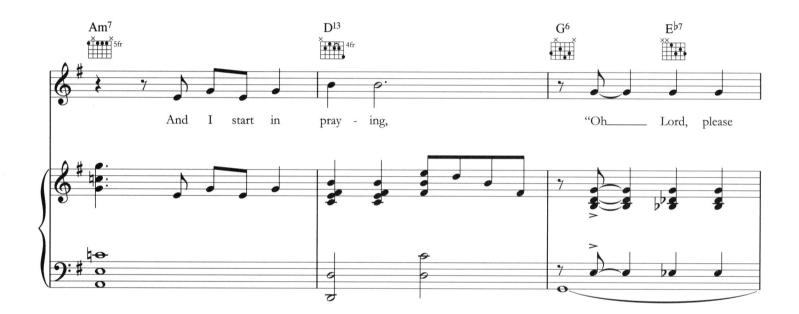

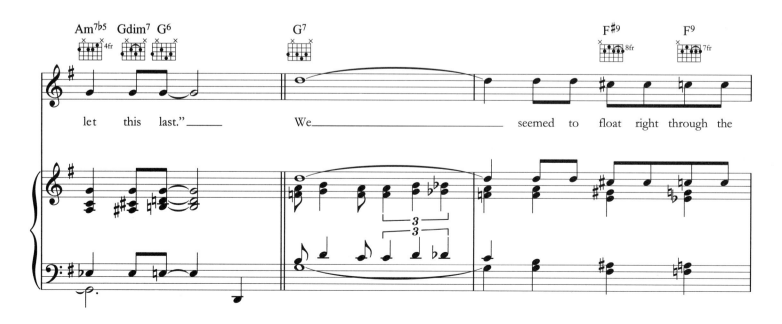

air. _____ Hea - ven - ly songs _____

_____ seemed to come from ev - - 'ry - where.

And now when there's moon - glow, way up in the

blue,

I al-ways re-mem-ber

that＿ moon-glow gave me you.＿

gave me you.＿

The More I See You

Lyrics by Mack Gordon
Music by Harry Warren

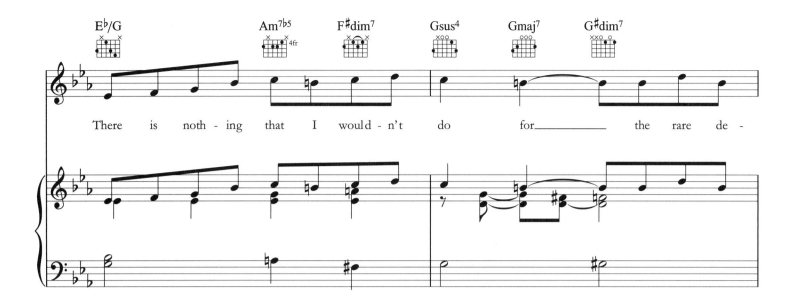

There is noth-ing that I would-n't do for_____ the rare de-

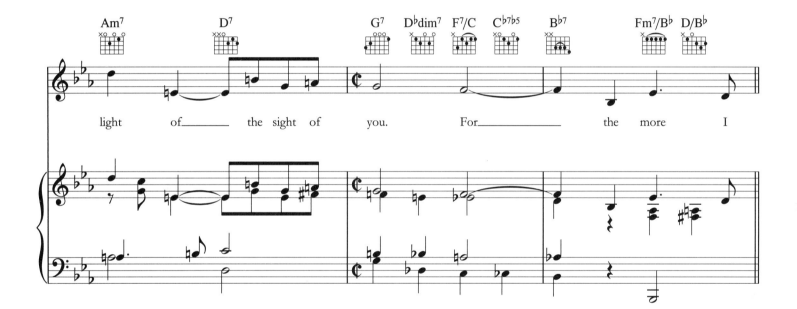

light of_____ the sight of you. For_____ the more I

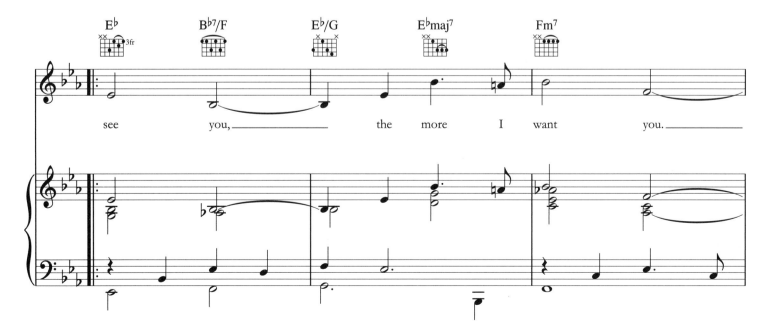

see you,_____ the more I want you._____

71

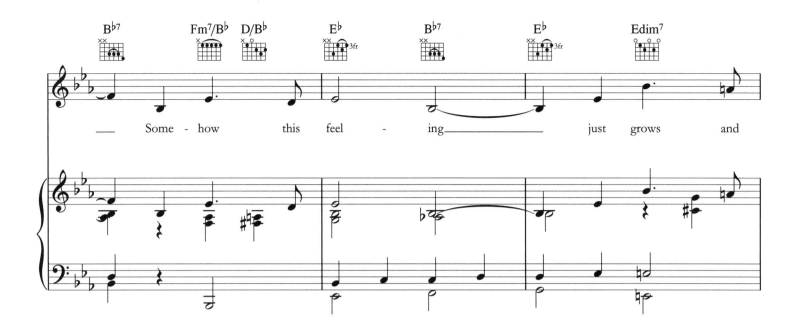

Some - how this feel - ing _____ just grows and

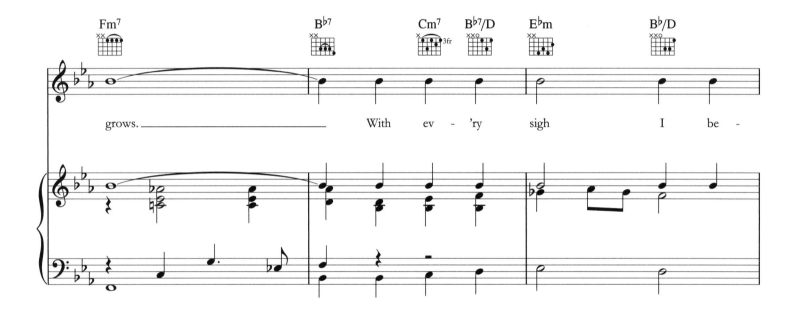

grows. _____ With ev - 'ry sigh I be -

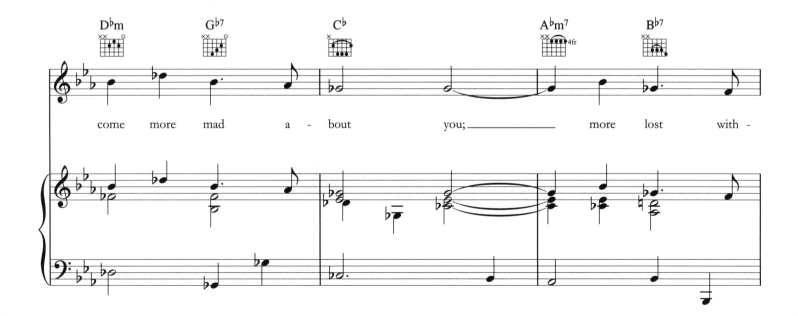

come more mad a - bout you; _____ more lost with -

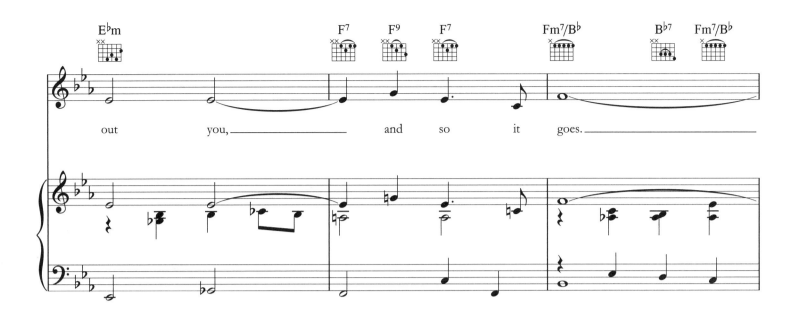

out you, and so it goes.

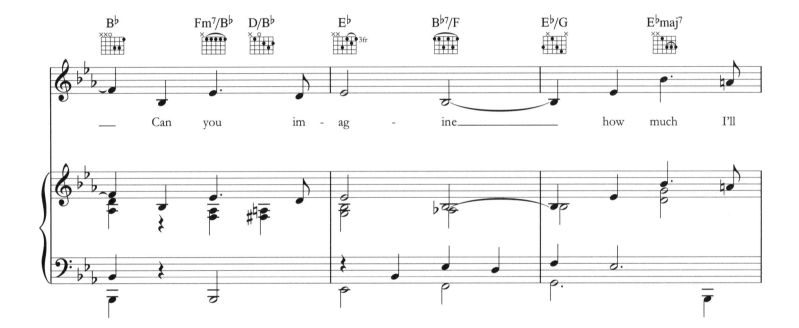

Can you im-ag - ine how much I'll

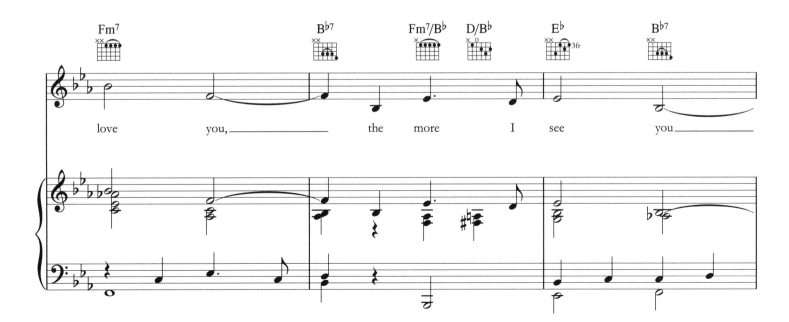

love you, the more I see you

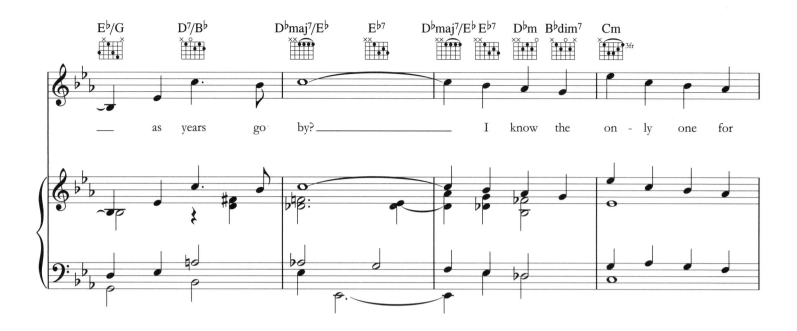

as years go by? _____ I know the on-ly one for

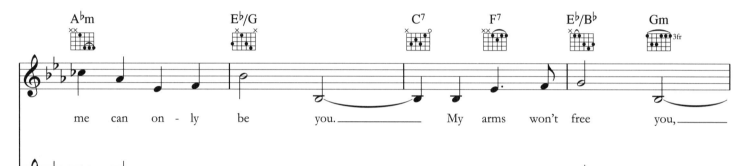

me can on-ly be you. _____ My arms won't free you, _____

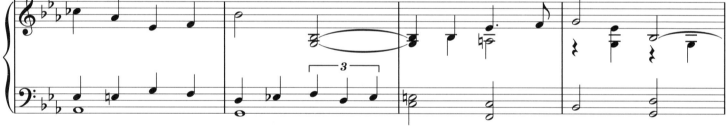

my heart won't try. _____ The more I try.

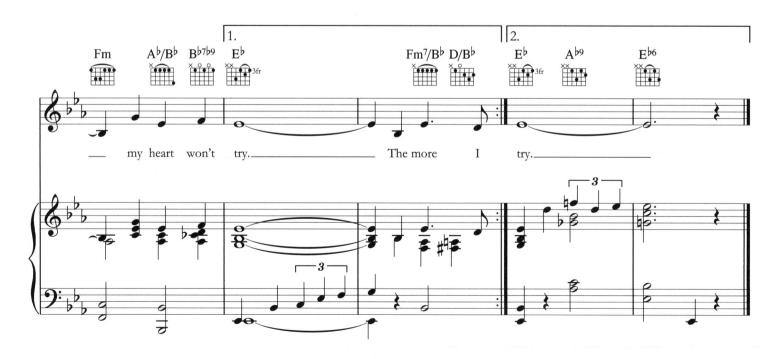

Sentimental Journey

Words and Music by Bud Green, Les Brown and Ben Homer

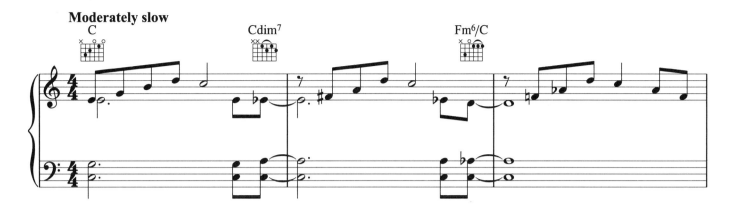

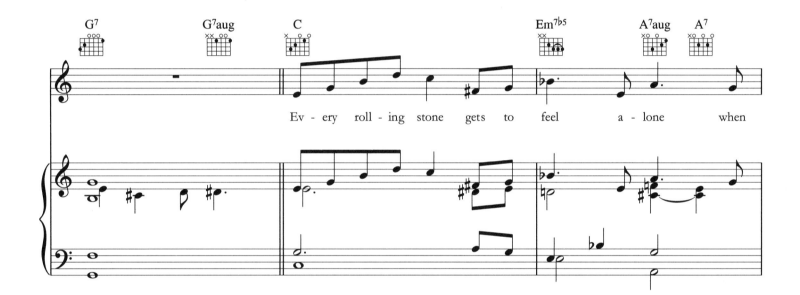

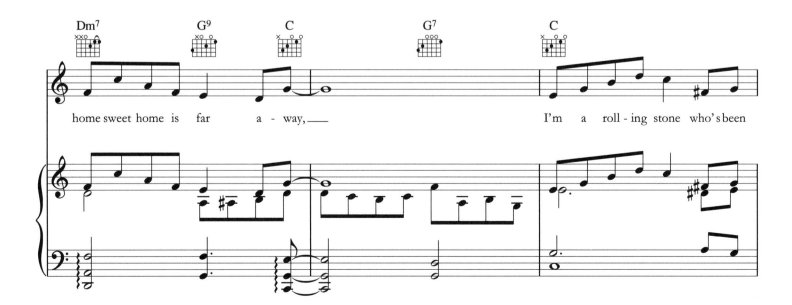

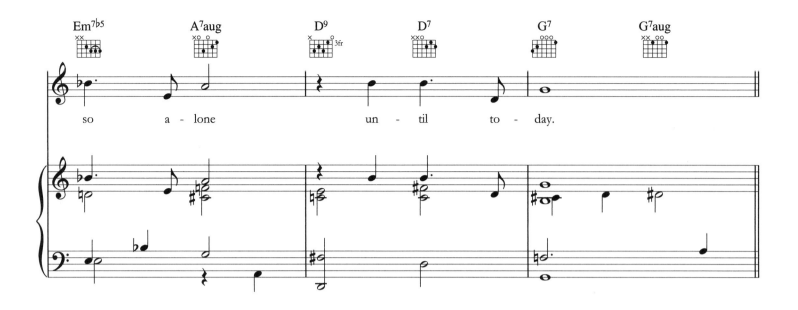

so a - lone   un - til to - day.

Gon - na take a sen - ti - men - tal jour - ney,   gon - na set my

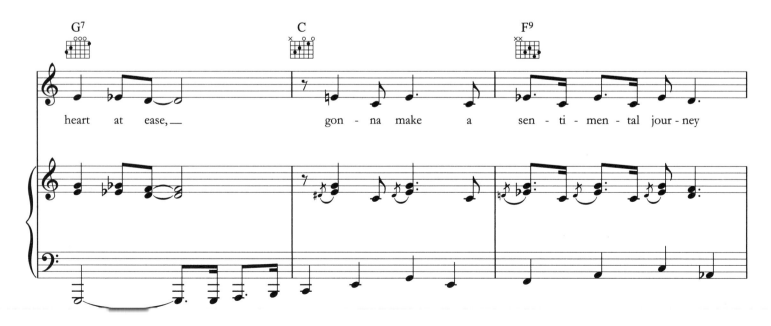

heart at ease, ___   gon - na make a sen - ti - men - tal jour - ney

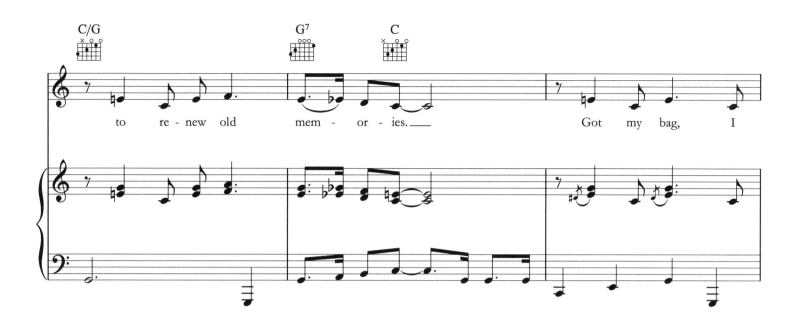

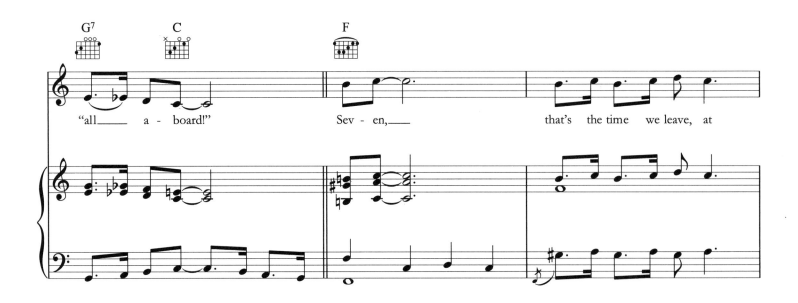

"all___ a - board!"   Sev - en,___   that's the time we leave, at

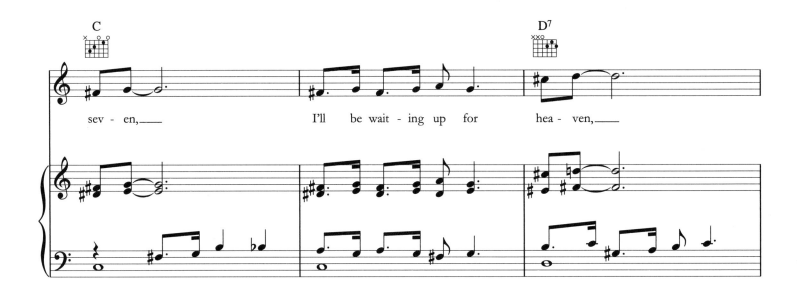

sev - en,___   I'll be wait - ing up for hea - ven,___

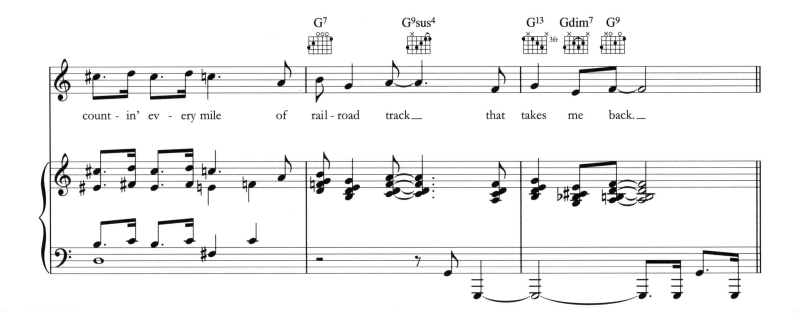

count - in' ev - ery mile of rail - road track___ that takes me back.___

Ne - ver thought my heart could be so year - ny, why did I de -

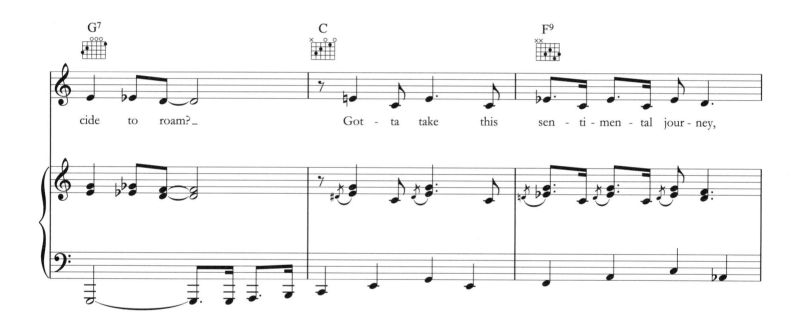

cide to roam?_ Got - ta take this sen - ti - men - tal jour - ney,

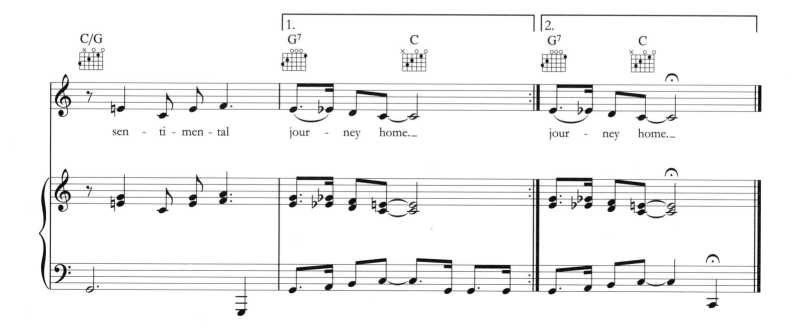

sen - ti - men - tal jour - ney home._ jour - ney home._

Oh Johnny, Oh Johnny, Oh!

Words by Ed Rose
Music by Abe Olman

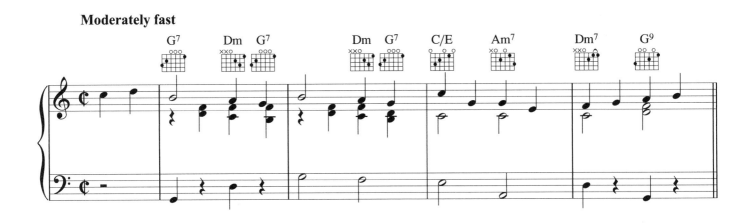

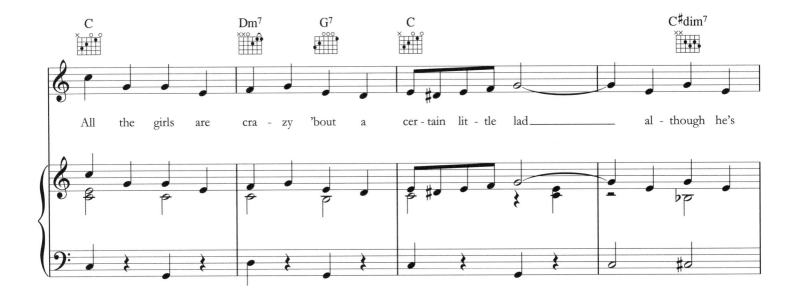

All the girls are cra-zy 'bout a cer-tain lit-tle lad_____ al-though he's

ver-y, ver-y bad,_____ he could be, oh so good when he want-ed to.

Bad or good he un - der - stood 'bout love and oth - er things,_____ for ev - 'ry

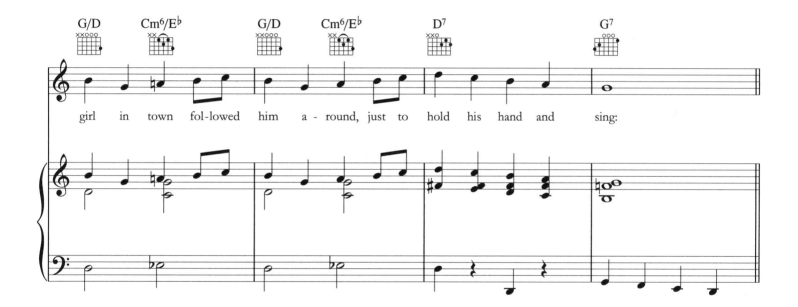

girl in town fol - lowed him a - round, just to hold his hand and sing:

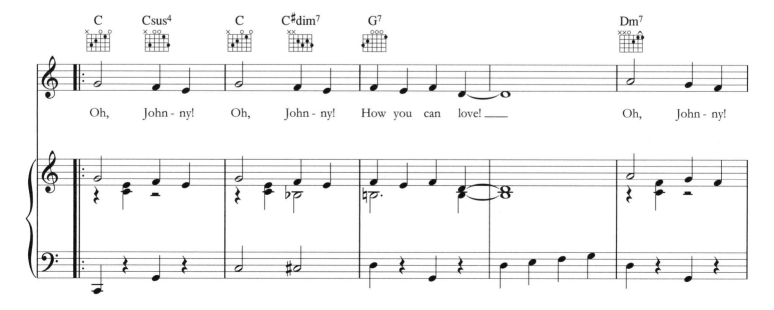

Oh, John - ny! Oh, John - ny! How you can love! ____ Oh, John - ny!

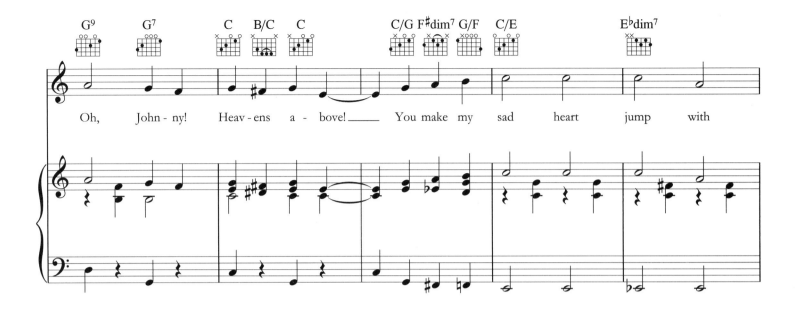

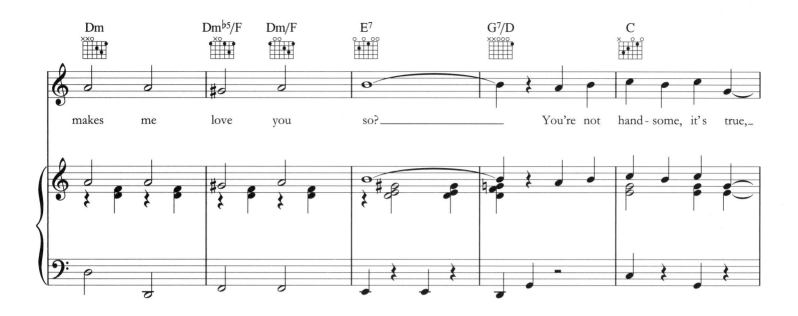

makes me love you so?_____ You're not hand - some, it's true,_

____ but when I look at you,_____ I just Oh, John - ny!

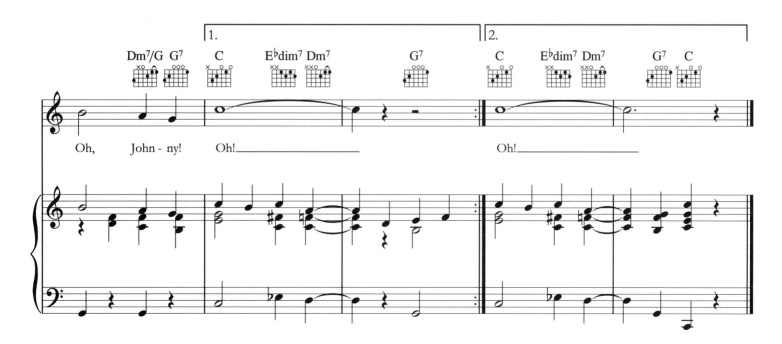

Oh, John - ny! Oh!_____ Oh!_____

On The Sunny Side Of The Street

Lyric by Dorothy Fields
Music by Jimmy McHugh

Moderato

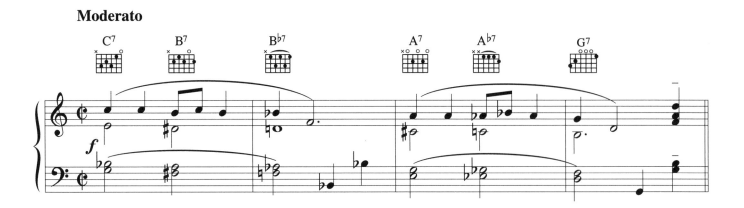

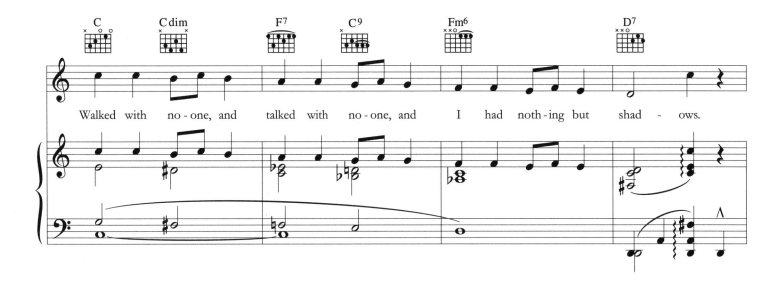

Walked with no-one, and talked with no-one, and I had noth-ing but shad - ows.

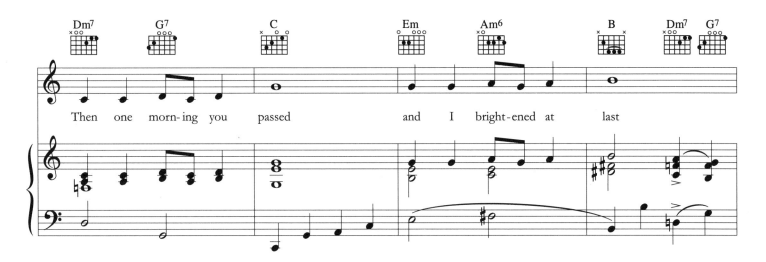

Then one morn-ing you passed and I bright-ened at last

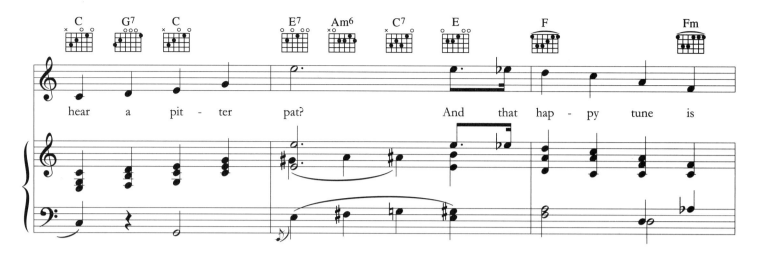

hear a pit - ter pat? And that hap - py tune is

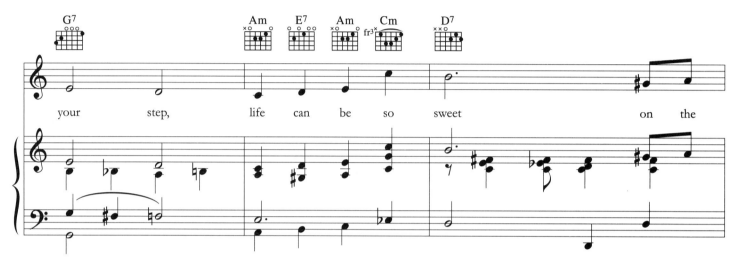

your step, life can be so sweet on the

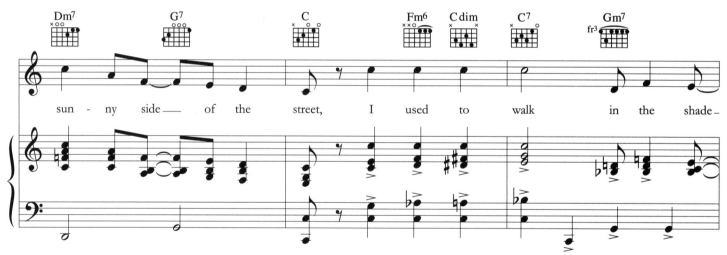

sun - ny side ___ of the street, I used to walk in the shade ___

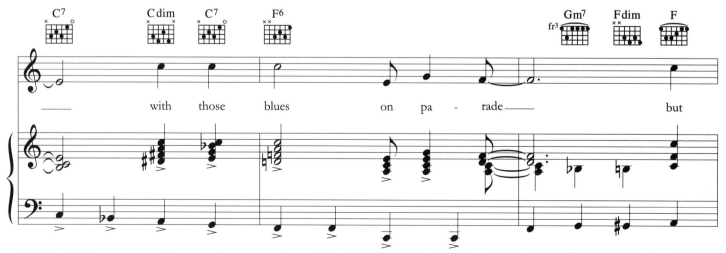

___ with those blues on pa - rade ___ but

September Song

(From the Musical Production *KNICKERBOCKER HOLIDAY*)

Words by Maxwell Anderson
Music by Kurt Weill

coup - le of whirls while I plied her with tears in lieu of pearls. And as time came a-round she
goods they bring they have lit - tle to of - fer but the songs they sing, and a plen - ti - ful waste of

came my way, as time came a-round she came.
time of day, a plen - ti - ful waste of time.

But it's a

long, long while from May to De - cem - ber,___ and the days grow

89

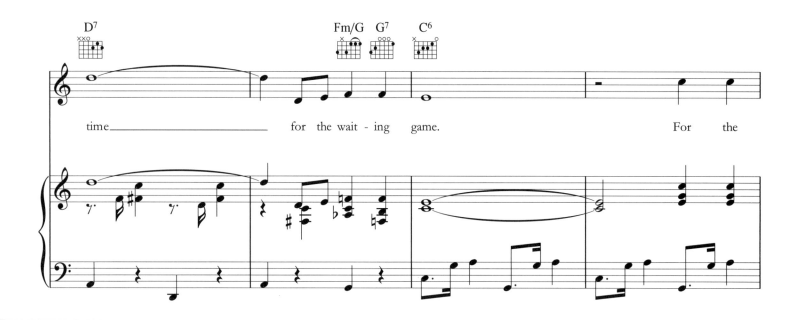

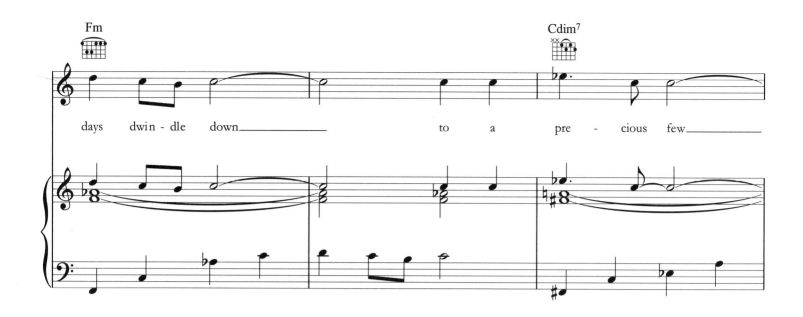

days dwin-dle down_____ to a pre-cious few_____

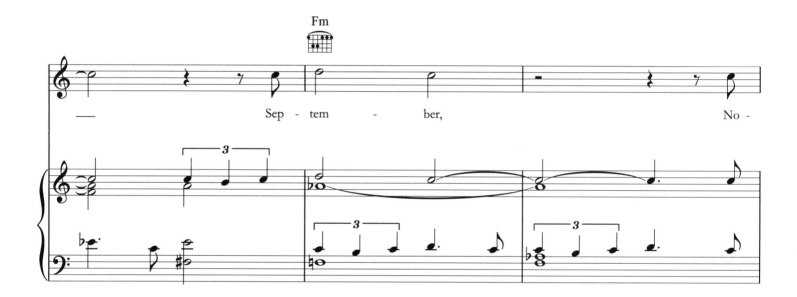

_ Sep -tem -ber, No -

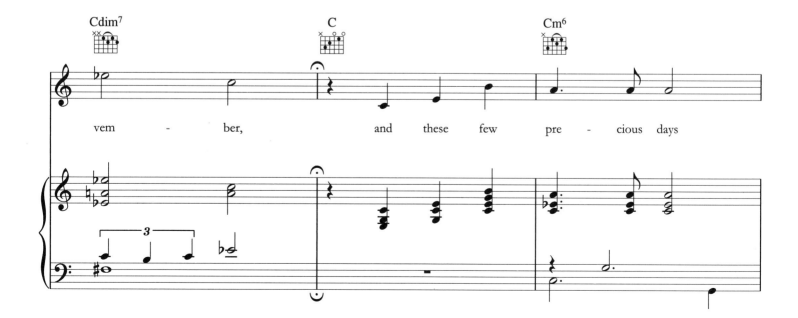

vem -ber, and these few pre -cious days

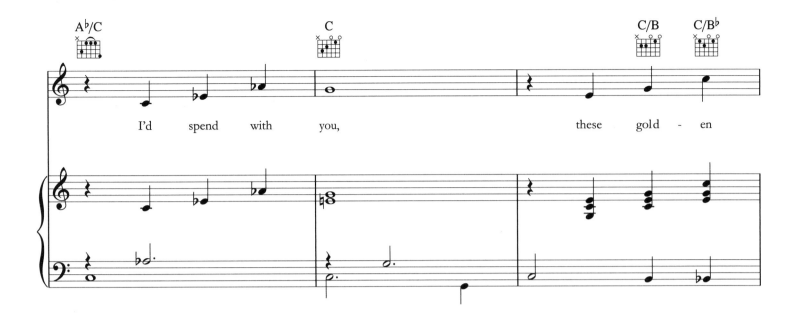

I'd spend with you, these gold - en

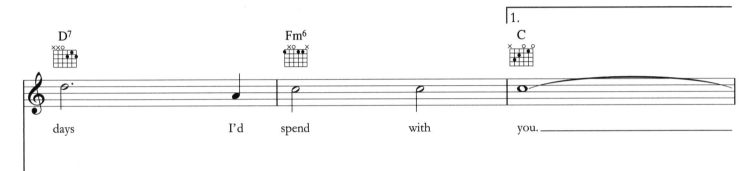

days I'd spend with you.

But it's a you.

Smoke Gets In Your Eyes

(from *ROBERTA*)

Words by Otto Harbach

Music by Jerome Kern

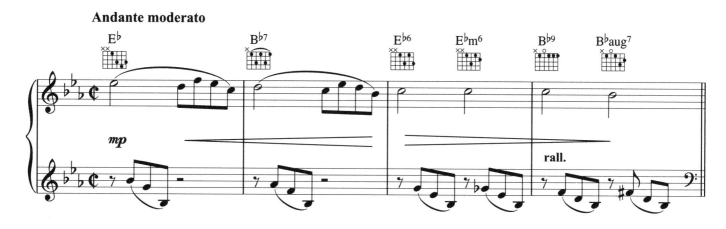

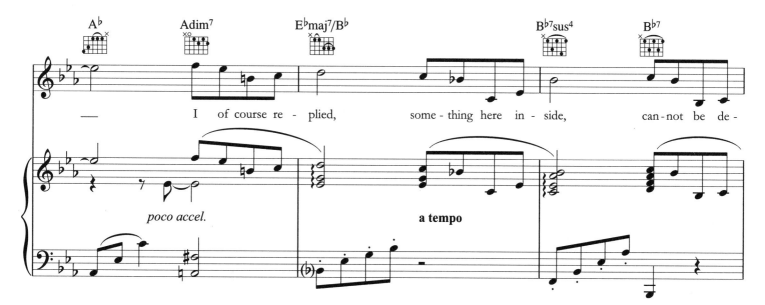

Take The "A" Train

By Billy Strayhorn

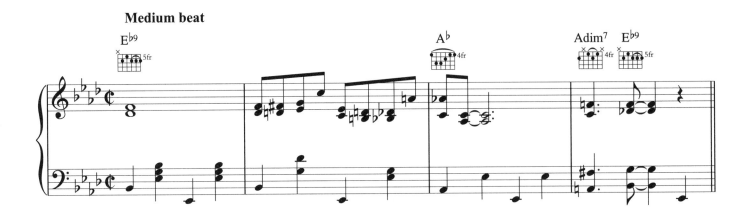

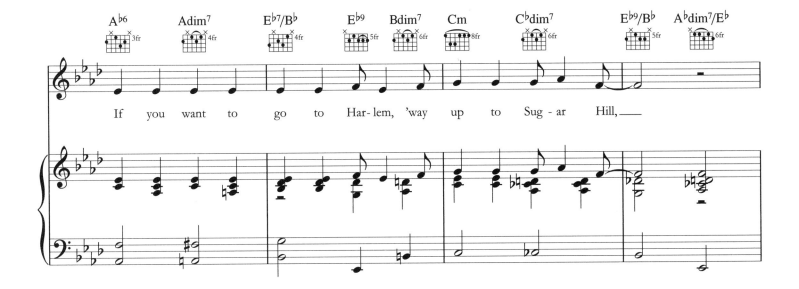

If you want to go to Har - lem, 'way up to Sug - ar Hill,___

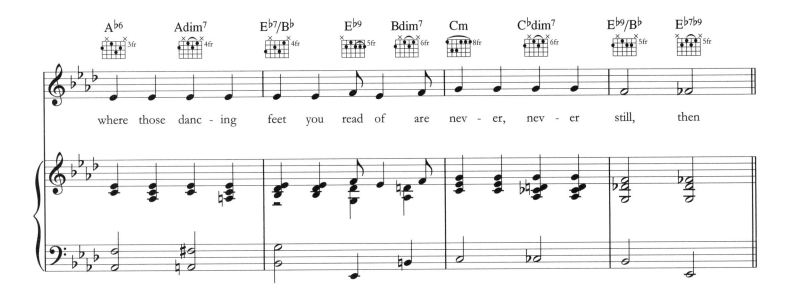

where those danc - ing feet you read of are nev - er, nev - er still, then

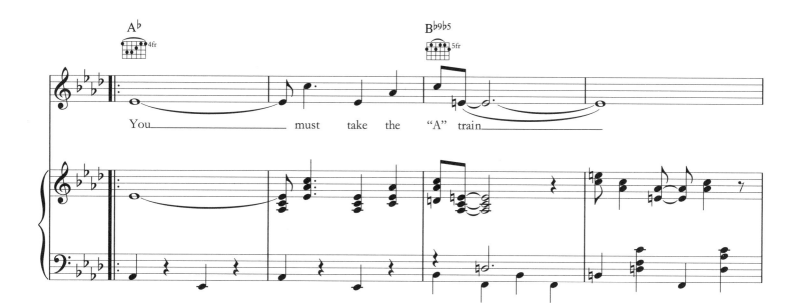

you'll   find you've missed the quick - est way to

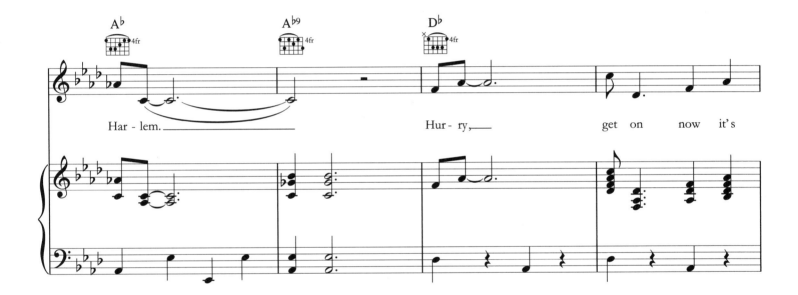

Har - lem.   Hur - ry,   get on now it's

com - ing   lis - ten   to those rails a -

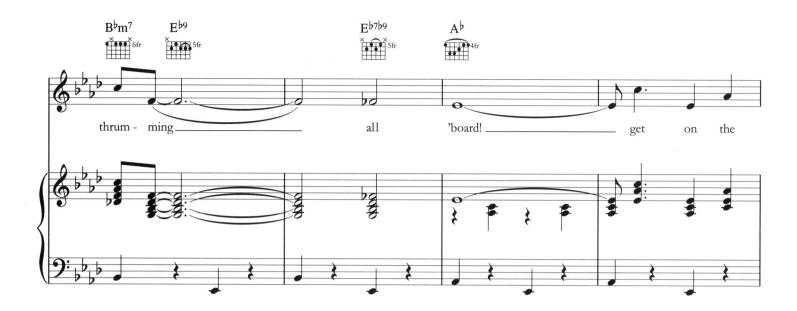

thrum - ming _____ all 'board! _____ get on the

"A" train _____ soon you will be on Sug - ar Hill in

1. Har - lem. _____

2. Har - lem. _____

Tangerine

(from the Paramount Picture *THE FLEET'S IN*)

Words by Johnny Mercer
Music by Victor Schertzinger

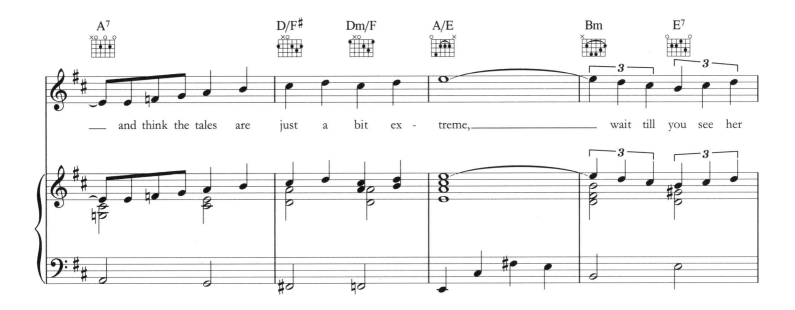

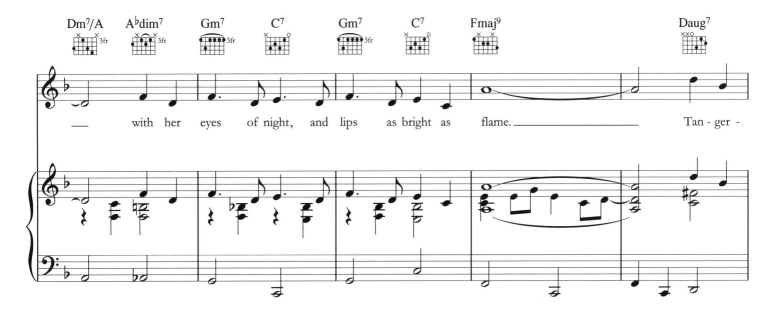

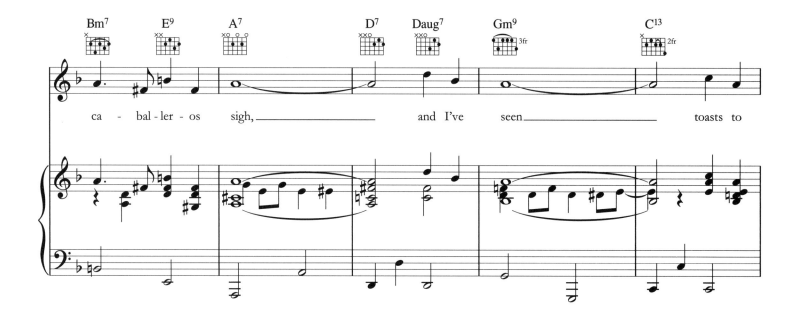

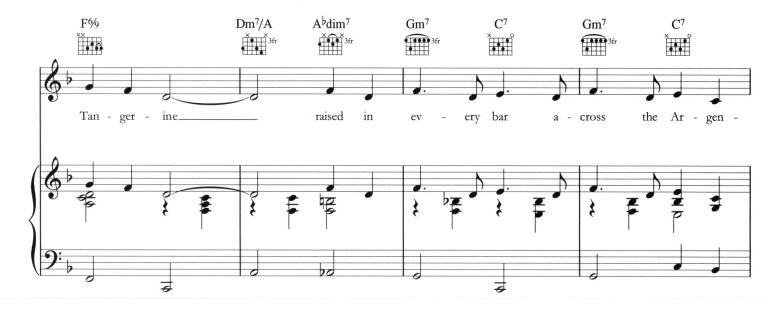

102

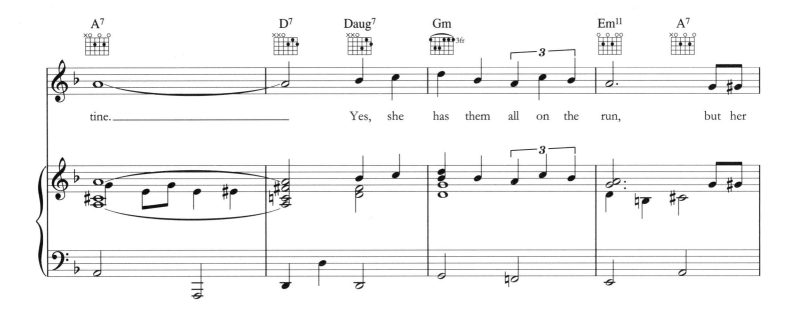

tine._____ Yes, she has them all on the run, but her

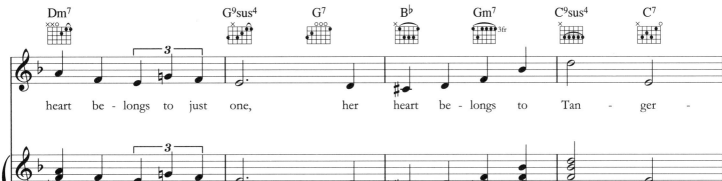

heart be - longs to just one, her heart be - longs to Tan - ger -

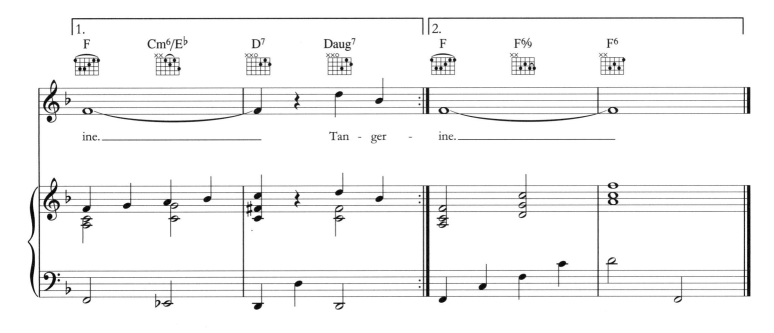

ine._____ Tan - ger - ine._____

Stormy Weather (Keeps Rainin' All The Time)

(from *COTTON CLUB PARADE OF 1933*)

Lyric by Ted Koehler

Music by Harold Arlen

What Is This Thing Called Love?

Words and Music by Cole Porter

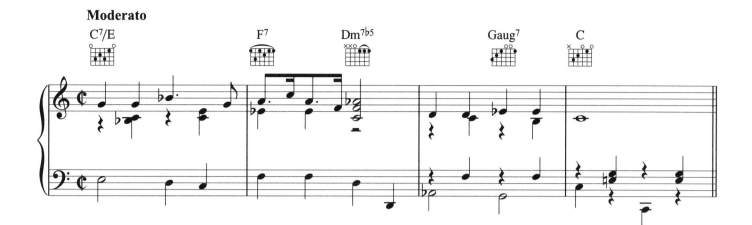

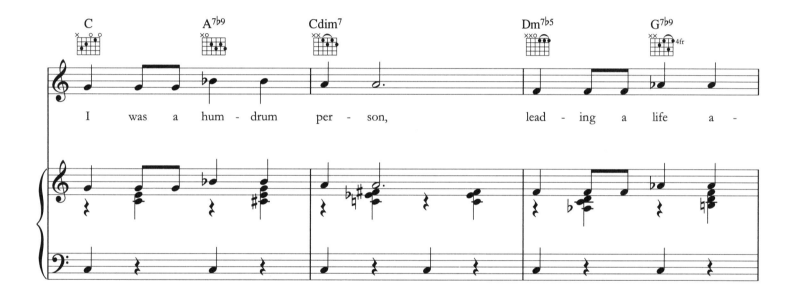

I was a hum-drum per-son, lead-ing a life a-

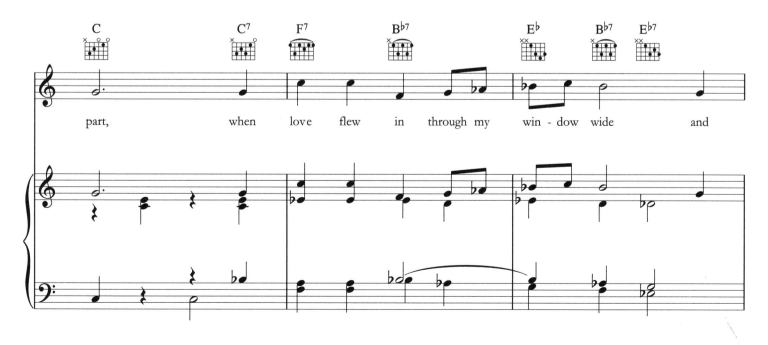

part, when love flew in through my win-dow wide and

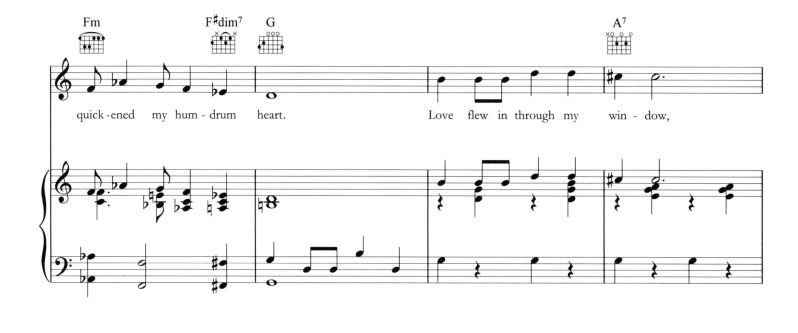

quick-ened my hum-drum heart. Love flew in through my win - dow,

I was so hap-py then. But af - ter love had stayed a lit - tle while,

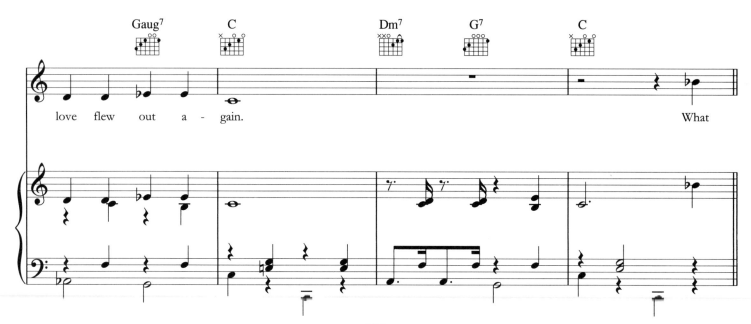

love flew out a - gain. What

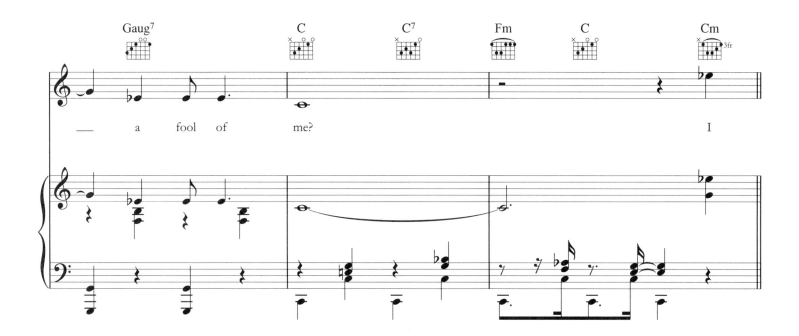

a fool of me? I

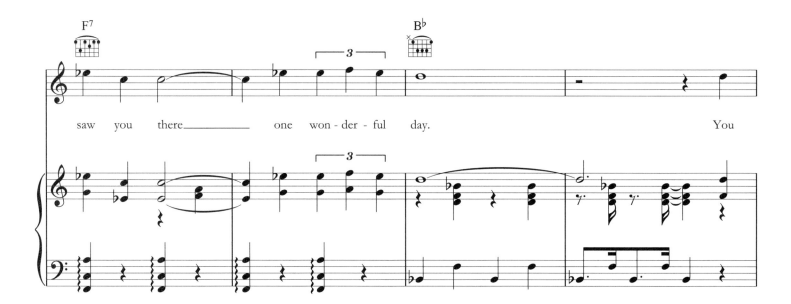

saw you there_____ one won - der - ful day. You

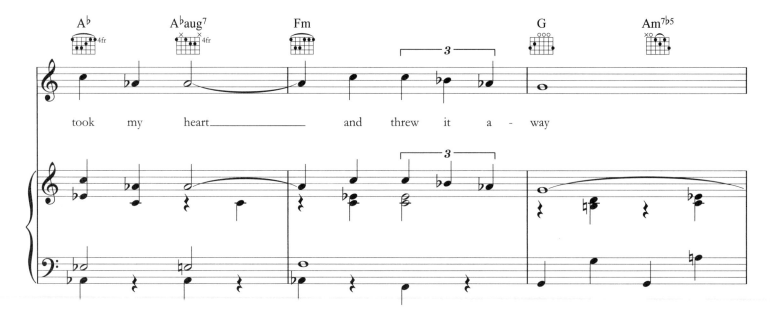

took my heart_____ and threw it a - way

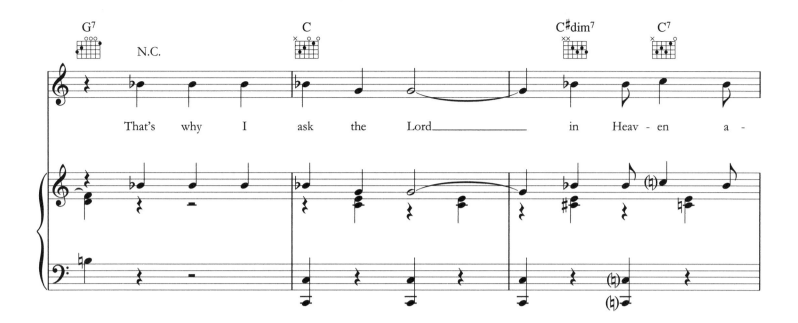

That's why I ask the Lord_____ in Heav-en a-

bove, what is this thing_____ called

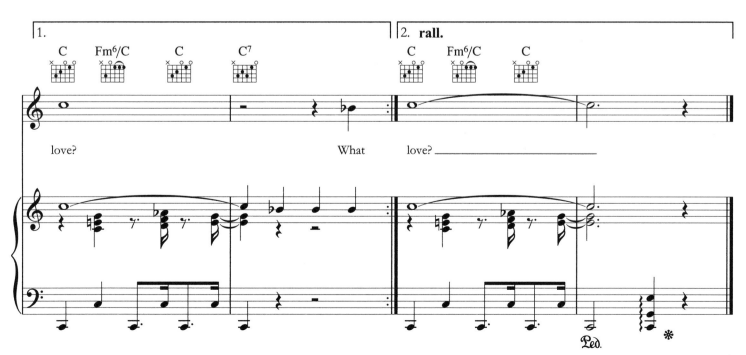

love? What love? _____

When You Wish Upon A Star

Words by Ned Washington

Music by Leigh Harline

You Go To My Head

Words by Haven Gillespie
Music by J. Fred Coots

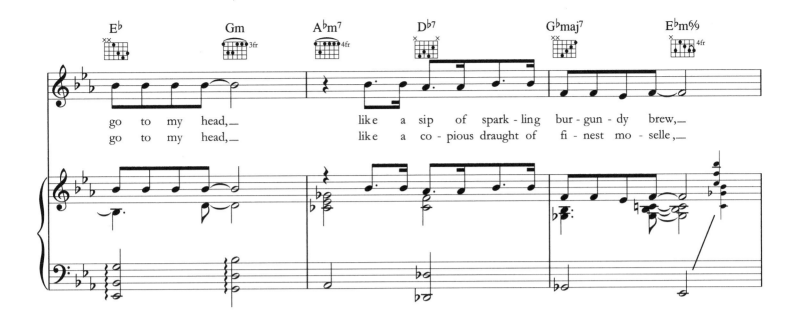

go to my head,—
go to my head,—
like a sip of spark-ling bur-gun-dy brew,—
like a co-pious draught of fi-nest mo-selle,—

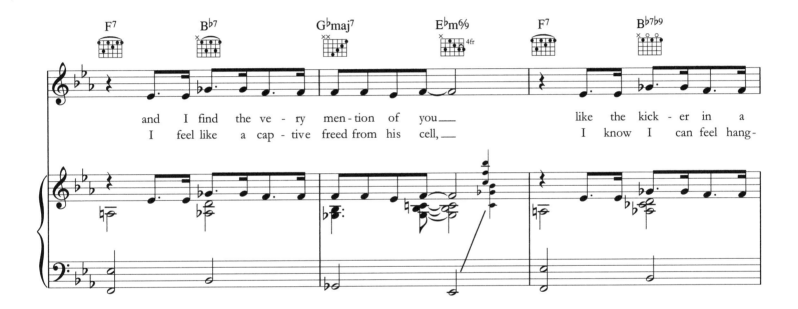

and I find the ve-ry men-tion of you___
I feel like a cap-tive freed from his cell,___
like the kick-er in a
I know I can feel hang-

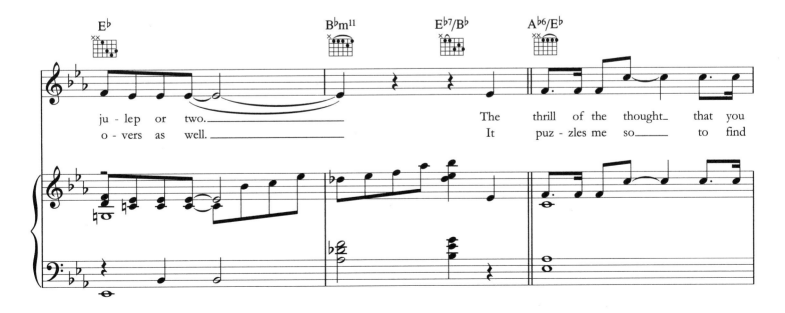

ju-lep or two.___
o-vers as well.___
The thrill of the thought___ that you
It puz-zles me so___ to find

might give a thought to my plea — casts a spell o - ver me.___ Still I
out if you know___ how you rule o'er the heart of a fool,___ and I

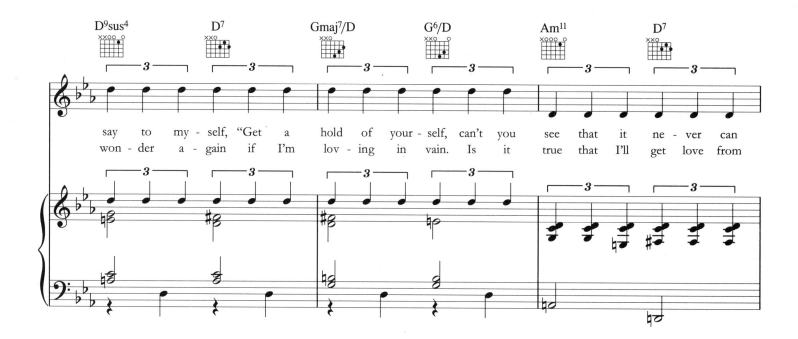

say to my - self, "Get a hold of your - self, can't you see that it ne - ver can
won - der a - gain if I'm lov - ing in vain. Is it true that I'll get love from

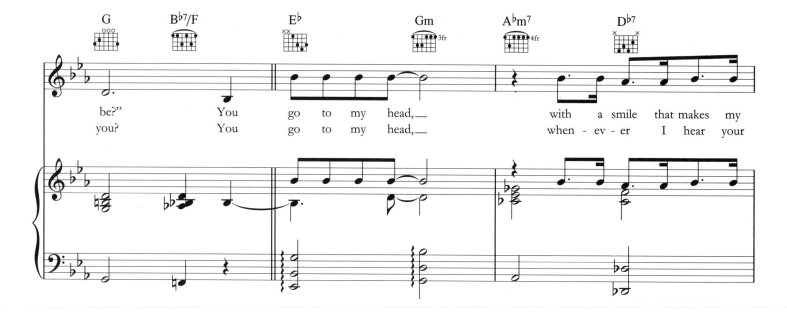

be?" You go to my head,___ with a smile that makes my
you? You go to my head,___ when - ev - er I hear your

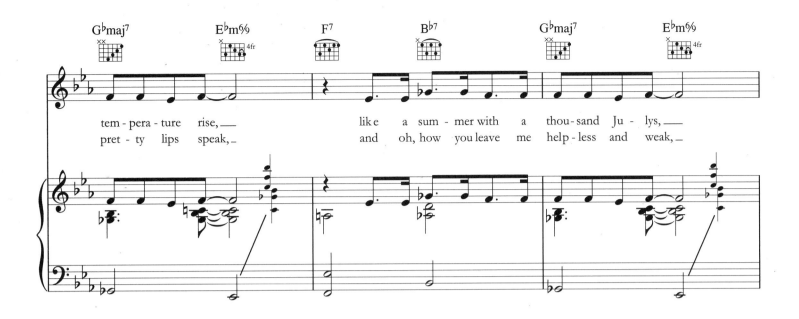

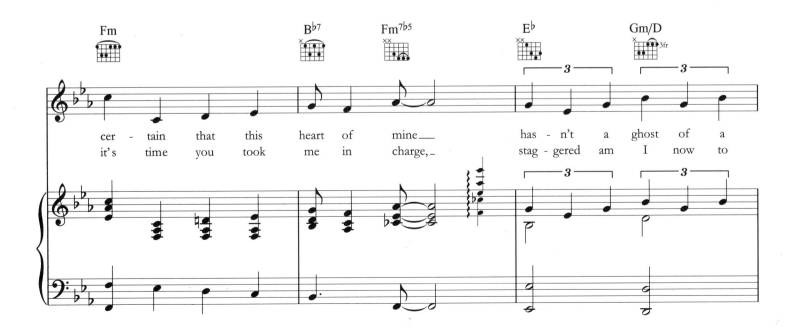

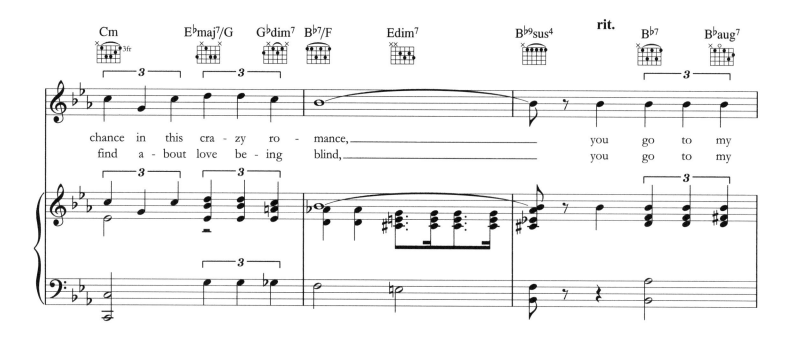

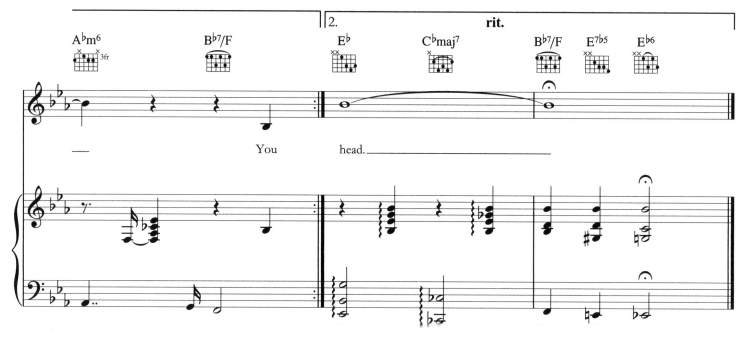

You Made Me Love You

Lyrics by Joe McCarthy
Music by James V. Monaco

You made me hap-py some - times, you made me glad, _____

but there were times dear, you made me feel___ so bad.___

You made me sigh for I did-n't want to tell you, I did-n't want to tell you.

You'd Be So Nice To Come Home To

Words and Music by Cole Porter

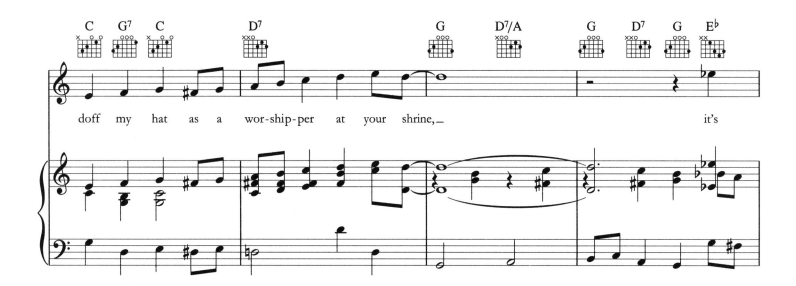

not that you're rar-er than as-par-a-gus out of sea-son, no, my

rit.

dar-ling, this is the reas-on why you've got to be___ mine. You'd be

a tempo

so nice___ to come home to,___

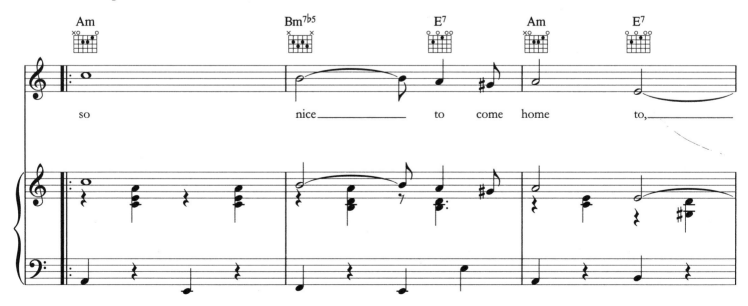

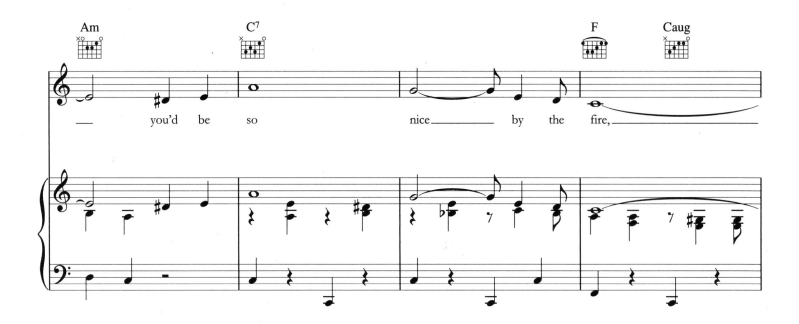

you'd be so nice_____ by the fire,_____

_____ while the breeze, on high,_____ sang a

lull - a - by,_____ you'd be all that I could de-

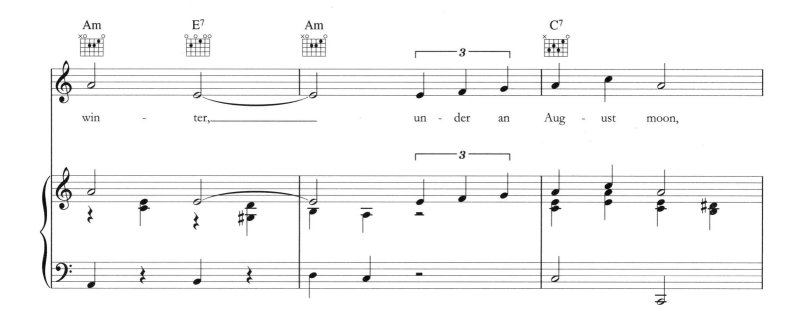

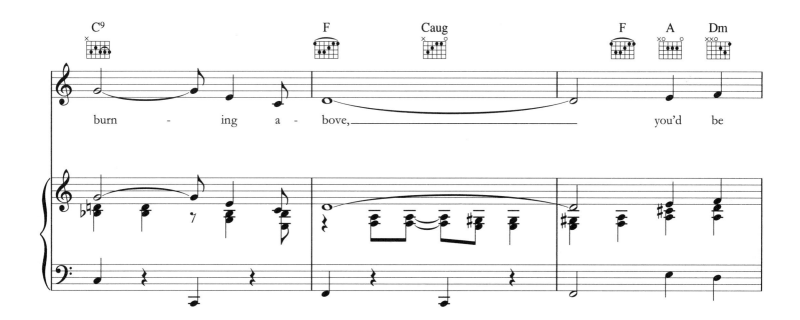